GRAPHIC ORGANIZERS
AND OTHER
VISUAL STRATEGIES

ENGAGE THE
BRAIN

MARCIA L. TATE

CORWIN PRESS
Classroom

For information:

Corwin Press
A SAGE Publications Company
2455 Teller Road
Thousand Oaks, California 91320
CorwinPress.com

SAGE Publications, Ltd.
1 Oliver's Yard
55 City Road
London EC1Y 1SP
United Kingdom

SAGE Publications India Pvt. Ltd.
B 1/I 1 Mohan Cooperative
Industrial Area
Mathura Road, New Delhi
India 110 044

SAGE Publications Asia-Pacific Pvt. Ltd.
33 Pekin Street #02-01
Far East Square
Singapore 048763

Printed in the United States of America.

ISBN 978-1-4129-5227-9

This book is printed on acid-free paper.

08 09 10 11 12 10 9 8 7 6 5 4 3 2 1

Executive Editor: Kathleen Hex
Managing Developmental Editor: Christine Hood
Editorial Assistant: Anne O'Dell
Developmental Writer: Susan Hodges
Developmental Editor: Kristine Johnson
Proofreader: Bette Darwin
Art Director: Anthony D. Paular
Cover Designer: Monique Hahn
Interior Production Artist: Karine Hovsepian
Illustrator: Jamie Smith
Design Consultant: PUMPKiN PIE Design

TABLE OF CONTENTS

Connections to Standards

This chart shows the national academic standards that are covered in each chapter.

MATHEMATICS	Standards are covered on pages
Numbers and Operations—Understand numbers, ways of representing numbers, relationships among numbers, and number systems.	15, 18 20
Numbers and Operations—Understand meanings of operations and how they relate to one another.	9, 12
Numbers and Operations—Compute fluently and make reasonable estimates.	9, 12
Geometry—Analyze characteristics and properties of two- and three-dimensional geometric shapes, and develop mathematical arguments about geometric relationships.	21, 23
Measurement—Understand measurable attributes of objects and the units, systems, and processes of measurement.	26
Measurement—Apply appropriate techniques, tools, and formulas to determine measurements.	26
Communication—Organize and consolidate mathematical thinking through communication.	20
Communication—Use the language of mathematics to express mathematical ideas precisely.	20
Connections—Recognize and use connections among mathematical ideas.	15
Connections—Understand how mathematical ideas interconnect and build on one another to produce a coherent whole.	15

SCIENCE	Standards are covered on pages
Science as Inquiry—Ability to conduct scientific inquiry.	35, 44
Science as Inquiry—Understand about scientific inquiry.	35, 44
Physical Science—Understand properties of objects and materials.	37
Physical Science—Understand light, heat, electricity, and magnetism.	40
Life Science—Understand characteristics of organisms.	30, 32
Life Science—Understand organisms and environments.	35
Earth and Space Science—Understand properties of earth materials.	42
Earth and Space Science—Identify objects in the sky.	46
Earth and Space Science—Understand changes in the earth and sky.	44

SOCIAL STUDIES	Standards are covered on pages
Understand culture and cultural diversity.	54, 56, 59
Understand the ways human beings view themselves in and over time.	50
Understand the interactions among people, places, and environments.	48, 50, 54
Understand individual development and identity.	62
Understand interactions among individuals, groups, and institutions.	56
Understand how people organize for the production, distribution, and consumption of goods and services.	52
Understand relationships among science, technology, and society.	60
Understand global connections and interdependence.	59

LANGUAGE ARTS	Standards are covered on pages
Read a wide range of print and nonprint texts to build an understanding of texts, of self, and of the cultures of the United States and the world; to acquire new information; to respond to the needs and demands of society and the workplace; and for personal fulfillment (includes fiction and nonfiction, classic, and contemporary works).	64, 74
Read a wide range of literature from many periods in many genres to build an understanding of the many dimensions (e.g., philosophical, ethical, aesthetic) of human experience.	74
Apply a wide range of strategies to comprehend, interpret, evaluate, and appreciate texts. Draw on prior experience, interactions with other readers and writers, knowledge of word meaning and of other texts, word identification strategies, and understanding of textual features (e.g., sound-letter correspondence, sentence structure, context, graphics).	64, 68, 71, 74, 82
Adjust the use of spoken, written, and visual language (e.g., conventions, style, vocabulary) to communicate effectively with variety of audiences and for different purposes.	71, 79
Employ a wide range of strategies while writing, and use different writing process elements appropriately to communicate with different audiences for a variety of purposes.	67, 76, 79
Apply knowledge of language structure, language conventions (e.g., spelling and punctuation), media techniques, figurative language, and genre to create, critique, and discuss print and nonprint texts.	67, 74, 82

Introduction

An ancient Chinese proverb claims: "Tell me, I forget. Show me, I remember. Involve me, I understand." This timeless saying insinuates what all educators should know: Unless students are involved and actively engaged in learning, true learning rarely occurs.

The latest brain research reveals that both the right and left hemispheres of the brain should be engaged in the learning process. This is important because the hemispheres talk to one another over the corpus callosum, the structure that connects them. No strategies are better designed for this purpose than graphic organizers and visuals. Both of these strategies engage students' visual modality. More information goes into the brain visually than through any other modality. Therefore, it makes sense to take advantage of students' visual strengths to reinforce and make sense of learning.

How to Use This Book

The activities in this book cover the content areas and are designed using strategies that actively engage the brain. They are presented in the way the brain learns best, to make sure students get the most out of each lesson: focus activity, modeling, guided practice, check for understanding, independent practice, and closing. Go through each step to ensure that students will be fully engaged in the concept being taught and understand its purpose and meaning.

Each step-by-step activity provides one or more visual tools students can use to make important connections between related concepts, structure their thinking, organize ideas logically, and reinforce learning. Graphic organizers and visuals include: place-value models, bar graph, network tree, concrete models, picture chart, idea web, Venn diagram, T-chart, newspapers, tally chart, collages, word cards, matrix, posters, circle chart, and more!

These brain-compatible activities are sure to engage and motivate every student's brain in your classroom! Watch your students change from passive to active learners as they process visual concepts into learning that is not only fun, but also remembered for a lifetime.

Put It Into Practice

Lecture and repetitive worksheets have long been the traditional way of delivering knowledge and reinforcing learning. While some higher-achieving students may engage in this type of learning, educators now know that actively engaging students' brains is not a luxury, but a necessity if students are truly to acquire and retain content, not only for tests, but for life.

The 1990s were dubbed the Decade of the Brain, because millions of dollars were spent on brain research. Educators today should know more about how students learn than ever before. Learning style theories that call for student engagement have been proposed for decades, as evidenced by research such as Howard Gardner's theory of multiple intelligences (1983), Bernice McCarthy's 4MAT Model (1990), and VAKT (visual, auditory, kinesthetic, tactile) learning styles theories.

I have identified 20 strategies that, according to brain research and learning style theory, appear to correlate with the way the brain learns best. I have observed hundreds of teachers—regular education, special education, and gifted. Regardless of the classification or grade level of the students, exemplary teachers consistently use these 20 strategies to deliver memorable classroom instruction and help their students understand and retain vast amounts of content.

These 20 brain-based instructional strategies include the following:

1. Brainstorming and Discussion

2. Drawing and Artwork

3. Field Trips

4. Games

5. Graphic Organizers, Semantic Maps, and Word Webs

6. Humor

7. Manipulatives, Experiments, Labs, and Models

8. Metaphors, Analogies, and Similes

9. Mnemonic Devices

10. Movement

11. Music, Rhythm, Rhyme, and Rap

12. Project-based and Problem-based Instruction

13. Reciprocal Teaching and Cooperative Learning

14. Role Plays, Drama, Pantomimes, Charades

15. Storytelling

16. Technology

17. Visualization and Guided Imagery

18. Visuals

19. Work Study and Apprenticeships

20. Writing and Journals

This book features Strategy 5: Graphic Organizers, Semantic Maps, and Word Webs, and Strategy 18: Visuals. Both of these strategies focus on integrating the visual and verbal elements of learning. Picture thinking, visual thinking, and visual/spatial learning is the phenomenon of thinking through visual processing. Since 90% of the brain's sensory input comes from visual sources, it stands to reason that the most powerful influence on learners' behavior is concrete, visual images. (Jensen, 1994) In addition, linking verbal and visual images increases students' ability to store and retrieve information. (Ogle, 2000)

Graphic organizers are visual representations of linear ideas that benefit both left and right hemispheres of the brain. They assist us in making sense of information, enable us to search for patterns, and provide an organized tool for making important conceptual connections. Graphic organizers, also known as word webs or semantic, mind, and concept maps, can be used to plan lessons or present information to students. Once familiar with the technique, students should be able to construct their own graphic organizers, reflecting their understanding of the concepts taught.

Because we live in a highly visual world, using visuals as a teaching strategy makes sense. Each day, students are overwhelmed with images from video games, computers, and television. Visual strategies capitalize specifically on the one modality that many students use consistently and have developed extensively—the visual modality. Types of visuals include overheads, maps, graphs, charts, and other concrete objects and artifacts that clarify learning. Since so much sensory input comes from visual sources, pictures, words, and learning-related artifacts around the classroom take on exaggerated importance in students' brains. Visuals such as these provide learning support and constant reinforcement.

These memorable strategies help students make sense of learning by focusing on the ways the brain learns best. Fully supported by the latest brain research, these strategies provide the tools you need to boost motivation, energy, and most important, the academic achievement of your students.

CHAPTER 1

Mathematics

Target Addition and Multiplication: Fact Wheels

Materials
On Target with Facts reproducible

counters

Skills Objectives
Solve addition and multiplication problems.
Recall addition and multiplication facts.
Commit basic facts to memory.

Third-grade students must master the basic number facts for all four operations. Ease the process by presenting facts in an organized group and by assigning only a few facts at a time. One way to do this is to use **Fact Wheels**. The wheel's center displays the target operation (e.g., +6, x7), while the numbers surrounding the center provide the addends or factors. (See "Subtraction and Division Bowling" on page 12 for subtraction and division activities.)

Working with Addition
Third graders already are familiar with addition. The following activity will help them focus on the facts they still need to master.

1. Begin with a quick review of addition facts. Write *8 + 4, 6 + 5*, and *7 + 7* on the board. Have students state the sums aloud. Explain that memorizing addition facts is important for solving higher-level addition problems quickly.

2. Give students a copy of the **On Target with Facts reproducible (page 11)**, and display an overhead transparency of the page. Have students follow along on their reproducibles as you write +6 in the center of the first target.

3. Have students add 6 to each number around the target and write the sums on the outer ring. Later, have students check their work as you go over the answers and write the sums on the transparency.

4. Direct the class to make three more sets of addition facts with the remaining targets. Assign specific

numbers, or let students pick their own. As students work, check to make sure they are filling in their targets correctly.

5. Later, have each student trade papers with a partner. Instruct partners to use their papers to quiz each other on the facts. For extra practice and reinforcement, have students make flashcards of the facts on their targets. They can practice the facts at home, one set at a time.

Working with Multiplication

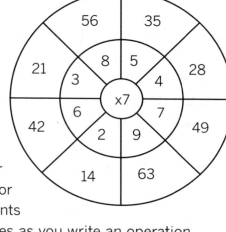

1. Review multiplication by writing *3 x 5* on the board. Ask a volunteer to draw small circles showing the expression (three groups of five circles). Remind students that the first number tells how many groups there are, while the second number tells how many are in each group.

2. Give students another copy of the On Target with Facts reproducible, and display a transparency of the page. Select four numbers for the targets' centers, such as consecutive numbers (2, 3, 4, 5), numbers whose products produce patterns (2, 5, 10, 11), or numbers that are often difficult for students (7, 8, 9, 12). Have students follow along on their reproducibles as you write an operation (e.g., *x7*) in the center of each target.

3. Have students write the products in the outer ring of the first target. Let them use counters or draw pictures if they need help. Students can check their work as you go over the answers and write them on the transparency. Direct the class to fill in the remaining targets.

4. Afterward, pair up students, and have partners quiz each other on the facts. For extra practice and reinforcement, have students make flashcards of the facts on their targets. They can practice the facts at home, one set at a time.

Name _____ Date _____

On Target with Facts

Directions: Write a number and operation in the center of each target. Then write the answers in the outer ring.

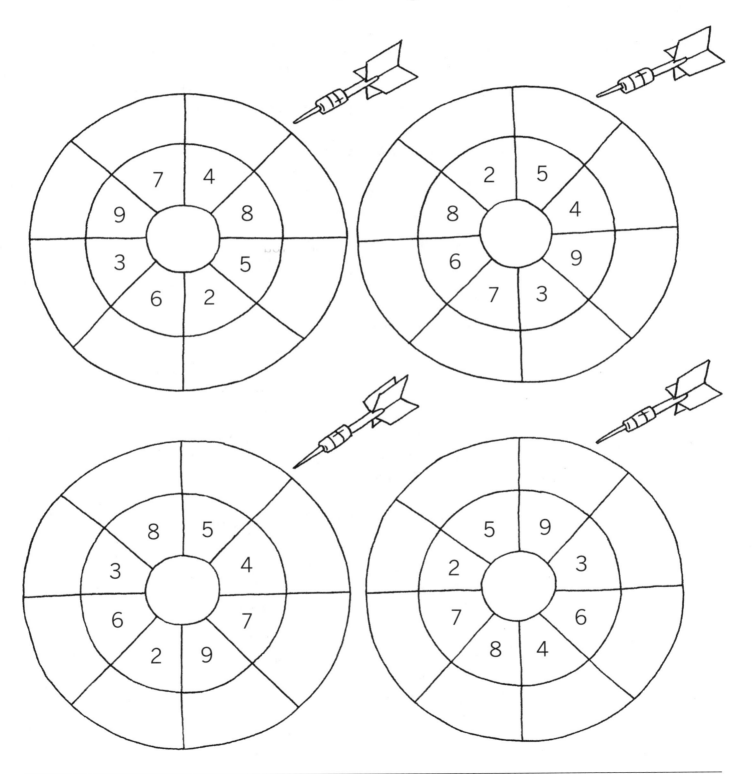

Subtraction and Division Bowling: Cluster

Materials
Bowling with Facts reproducible

counters

Skills Objectives
Solve subtraction and division problems.
Recall subtraction and division facts.
Commit basic facts to memory.

Subtraction and division facts can be difficult to master. Help students master these facts by encouraging them to focus on only a few facts at a time. Presenting the facts in a **Cluster**—a set made up of similar facts—can help students commit facts to memory.

Working with Subtraction
Third graders are familiar with the concept of subtraction, but some may not be able to recall the facts quickly. Help students apply their knowledge of addition facts to practice subtraction facts.

1. For a quick review, write a few subtraction problems on the board. Ask volunteers to provide the differences. Explain that memorizing subtraction facts can help when solving higher-level subtraction problems.

2. Show students how they can use their knowledge of addition facts to help master subtraction facts. Write *14 – 5* on the board. Ask students: *What plus 5 equals 14?* Help them see that the answer must be 9. Repeat the process with more facts that involve subtracting 5.

3. Give students a copy of the **Bowling with Facts reproducible (page 14)**, and display an overhead transparency of the page. Point to the ball and pins on the upper left. Write *–5* on the ball and have students do the same on their papers. Ask the class to suggest numbers between 5 and 15. Write them on the top half of each pin, while students follow along on their papers.

4. Tell students to subtract 5 from each number and write the answer on the bottom half of each pin. Let them use counters or pictures if they need help. Later, students can check their work as you review the answers.

5. Have students make three more sets of subtraction facts with the remaining balls and pins. Assign specific numbers to subtract or let students choose their own. Make sure students understand the task before they begin.

6. Afterward, ask students to trade papers with a partner so they can quiz each other on subtraction facts. For extra practice, students can make flashcards of their subtraction facts and practice the facts at home.

Working with Division

Division is a relatively new concept for third graders. After students experience dividing objects into groups, do this activity to help them master the facts.

1. Draw 24 small circles on the board, and circle them to form three equal groups. Write *24 ÷ 3* and ask students to state the answer (8). Then point to the picture and ask: *What times 3 equals 24?* Help students see that the answer is 8. Repeat the activity with 18 ÷ 3 and ask: *What times 3 equals 18?* Explain that it's helpful to think of corresponding multiplication facts when learning division facts.

2. Give students another copy of the Bowling with Facts reproducible, and display an overhead transparency of the page. Point to the ball and pins on the upper left. Write *÷3* on the ball, and have students write the same on their papers. Ask the class to brainstorm numbers that are divisible by 3 (these are actually products of 3). On the transparency, write these numbers on the top half of each pin, while students follow along on their papers.

3. Have students divide the number on each pin by 3 and write the quotient on the bottom half of each pin. Let students use counters or pictures if they need help. Students can check their work as you review the answers.

4. Have students make three more sets of division facts with the remaining balls and pins. Assign specific numbers or let students choose their own. Check to be sure that students understand the assignment before they begin the activity.

5. Later, pair up students and have partners quiz each other on division facts. For extra practice, students can make flashcards of their division facts and practice the facts at home.

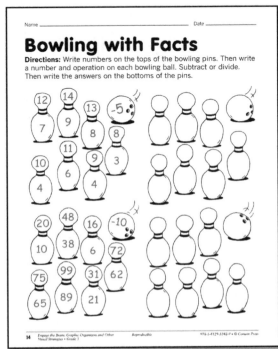

Bowling with Facts

Directions: Write numbers on the tops of the bowling pins. Then write a number and operation on each bowling ball. Subtract or divide. Then write the answers on the bottoms of the pins.

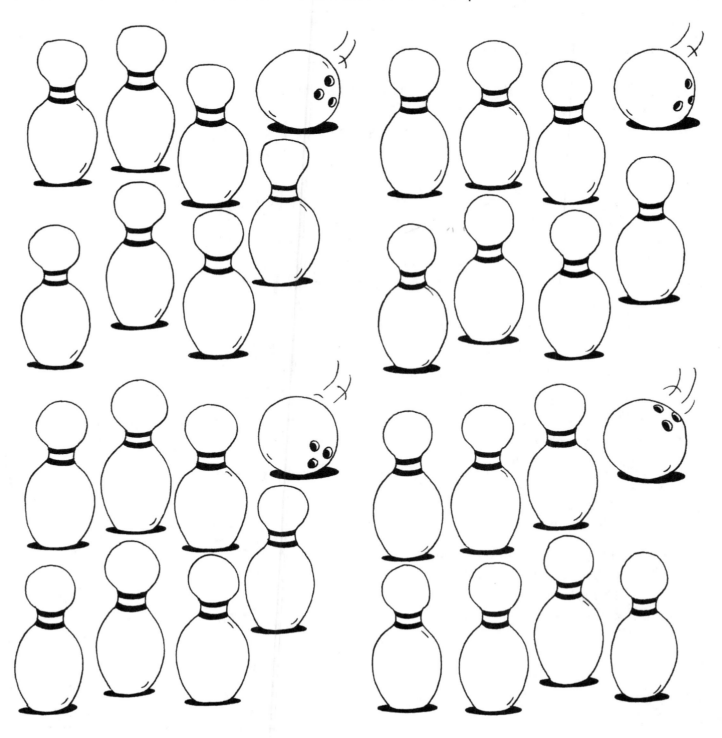

 Engage the Brain: Graphic Organizers and Other Visual Strategies • Grade 3   Reproducible   978-1-4129-5342-9 • © Corwin Press

Place-Value: Models and Charts

Skills Objectives
Recognize place-value groupings.
Understand that numbers are written based on place-value groupings.
Identify four-digit numbers based on the number of thousands, hundreds, tens, and ones.

In third grade, students begin working more extensively with large numbers. They need a firm foundation in place value and an understanding that our number system is built on groups of ten. Concrete **Place-Value Models** and **Place-Value Charts** are valuable tools for developing this skill. Commercially made products, such as cubes and rods, provide hands-on experiences that help students explore the connection between written numbers and the amounts they represent.

Materials
Place-Value Models reproducible

place-value models (thousand cubes, hundred flats, ten rods, unit cubes)

2 sheets of white butcher paper

light-colored butcher paper

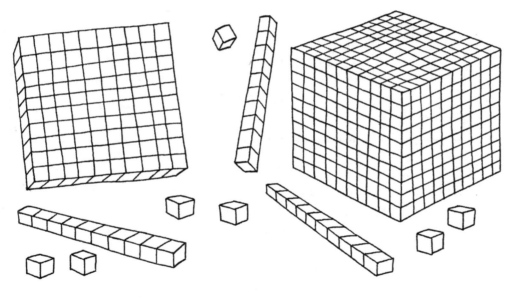

1. Review place value with students (the concept that the position of a digit indicates its value). Write *23* on the board, and ask a volunteer to arrange place-value models to match (2 ten rods and 3 unit cubes). Set out 2 hundred flats and 3 unit cubes, and ask why that amount does not match 23. Explain that the *2* in *23* represents tens, not hundreds.

2. Draw two place-value charts on separate sheets of white butcher paper. For each chart, make five columns: *Thousands, Hundreds, Tens, Ones,* and *We Write*. Place Chart 1 on a table, and ask students to stand around it. Post Chart 2 nearby.

3. Place a unit cube in the ones column on Chart 1. Ask how many cubes there are. Write *1* in the ones column on Chart 2, and *1* in

the We Write column on both charts to indicate how the amount is written.

4. Start adding cubes one at a time to the ones column while the class counts aloud. Stop when there are 10. Remind the class that 10 ones should be replaced by 1 ten. Remove the cubes, and replace them with a rod in the tens column on Chart 1. Fill in the tens and ones column on Chart 2, and write *10* in the We Write columns on both charts.

Thousands	Hundreds	Tens	Ones	We Write
				1
				10
				100
				1,000

5. Add rods one at a time to the tens column, and have students count the cubes by tens (e.g., *10, 20, 30*) until you have 100. Replace the 10 ten rods with a hundred flat, and fill in the hundreds, tens, and ones columns on Chart 2. Then write *100* in the We Write columns. Repeat the procedure for 1,000, stacking the hundred flats and eventually replacing them with a thousand cube. Explain that 10 hundreds form a group called "one thousand."

6. Divide the class into small groups, and give each group several copies of the **Place-Value Models reproducible (page 17)**. Tell groups to cut out the models and arrange place-value groupings on a sheet of light-colored butcher paper. Below each grouping, students write the number of thousands, hundreds, tens, and ones, along with the matching number. Display students' completed work.

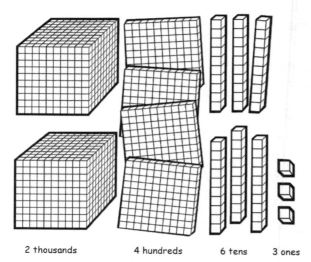

2 thousands   4 hundreds   6 tens   3 ones

Place-Value Models

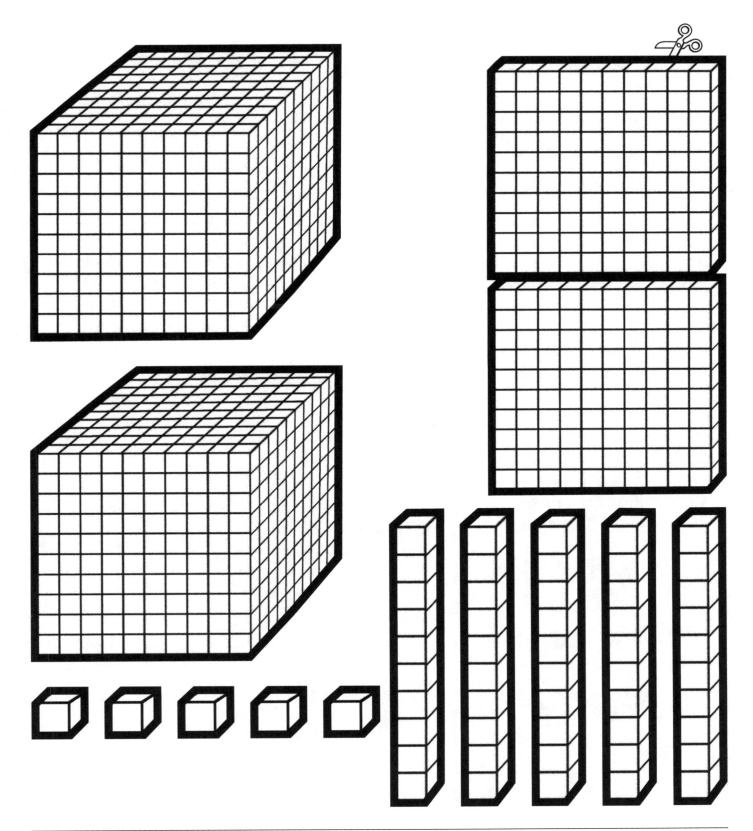

Caterpillar Fractions: Models

Materials

Caterpillar Fractions reproducible

2" paper circles (2 red, 3 yellow, 1 blue)

Skills Objectives

Read and write fractions.
Identify fractional parts of a group.

The concept of fractions can be challenging for students. Using **Models** provides hands-on experiences that help students develop a deeper understanding of concepts. These models illustrate abstract ideas in a concrete, visual way that makes sense.

1. Ahead of time, make a paper caterpillar by gluing two red circles, three yellow circles, and one blue circle onto a sheet of paper. Add facial features and a pair of antennae.

2. Show the caterpillar to the class. Have students count the circles. (6) Ask how many circles are red. (2) Have students state the fraction that tells what portion of the caterpillar is red. Write 2/6 on the board. Point out that the *numerator* on top tells how many circles are red; the *denominator* on the bottom tells how many circles there are in all.

3. Repeat this procedure to help students see that 3/6 of the caterpillar is yellow and 1/6 is blue.

4. Give students a copy of the **Caterpillar Fractions reproducible (page 19)**. Have them color the caterpillars and write fractions for each color. As they work, check for correct fractional parts.

5. Display completed caterpillars on a bulletin board titled *Caterpillar Fractions*.

Extended Learning

• Let students make their own caterpillars by gluing together colored paper circles. Have them write a fraction for each color of their caterpillar.

• Have students add up the fractions for each caterpillar (e.g., 1/9 + 3/9 + 5/9 = 9/9). Explain that when the numerator and denominator are the same number, the fraction equals one whole, or 1.

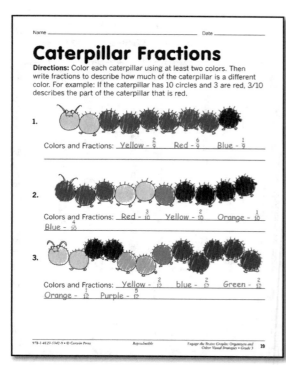

Name _____ Date _____

Caterpillar Fractions

Directions: Color each caterpillar using at least two colors. Then write fractions to describe how much of the caterpillar is a different color. For example: If the caterpillar has 10 circles and 3 are red, 3/10 describes the part of the caterpillar that is red.

1. Colors and Fractions: Yellow - 2/9   Red - 6/9   Blue - 1/9

2. Colors and Fractions: Red - 3/10   Yellow - 2/10   Orange - 1/10   Blue - 4/10

3. Colors and Fractions: Yellow - 2/12   blue - 2/12   Green - 2/12   Orange - 1/12   Purple - 5/12

Caterpillar Fractions

Directions: Color each caterpillar using at least two colors. Then write fractions to describe how much of the caterpillar is a different color. For example: If the caterpillar has 10 circles and 3 are red, 3/10 describes the part of the caterpillar that is red.

1.

Colors and Fractions: _____

_____

2.

Colors and Fractions: _____

_____

3.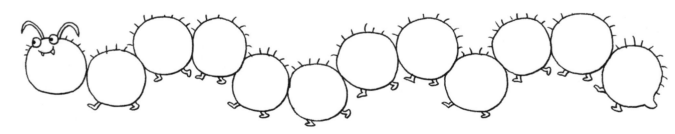

Colors and Fractions: _____

_____

Decimal Lineup: Number Line

Skills Objectives
Identify and sequence tenths on a number line.
Compare decimals on a number line.

A **Number Line** presents numbers in ascending order. Because numbers increase to the right and decrease to the left, the number line makes comparing numbers easy. In this activity, students use a number line to identify and compare tenths; it may be adapted to include hundredths. Do this activity after introducing the concept of decimals.

1. Draw a number line on the board. Draw 11 short vertical lines spaced evenly across the line. Label the first mark *0* and the last mark *1.0*. Explain that the area between 0 and 1.0 represents numbers greater than 0 but less than 1.

2. Label the first mark after zero *0.1*, and ask students to identify its value. *(one tenth)* Ask them to identify the values of the other markings, and call on volunteers to write the decimals on the number line.

3. Point to each mark as students count aloud: *zero, one tenth, two tenths*, and so on, until you reach *one*. Ask how counting tenths on the number line is similar to counting whole numbers. (Numbers become greater as you move to the right and increase one unit at a time. Whole numbers increase by 1; tenths increase by 1/10.)

4. Refer students to the number line while doing these activities:
   - Write *0.4* on the board. Have students state the decimal that comes before and after the number. Repeat with other tenths.
   - Write *0.5*, *0.2*, and *0.7* on the board. Ask a student to write the decimals in order, from least to greatest. Repeat with other sets of decimals.
   - Write *0.8* and *1.0*, and ask students to state the greater number. Repeat with other pairs of numbers.

5. As a follow-up, have students copy your number line, but label only half the marks. (Let students choose which marks to leave blank.) Tell them to trade papers with a partner, and fill in the missing decimals on their partner's paper.

Extended Learning
Extend the number line to include decimals greater than 1 (1.1, 1.2, and so on). Repeat the activities described in Step 4.

Plane Figures: Network Tree

Skills Objectives
Recognize attributes of plane figures.
Identify and classify plane figures.

Materials
Plane Figures
reproducible

chart paper

A **Network Tree** organizes information so the main topic splits into subtopics, with each subtopic splitting into more subtopics. A network tree lets students visualize how different ideas or concepts are interrelated. In this activity, students use a network tree to categorize various plane figures.

1. Draw two figures on the board: a square and a square that has a break in its outline. Ask how the two shapes are alike and different. Help students see that the two shapes are *plane figures* (flat shapes). The second figure is similar to the first except for the break in its outline. Explain that plane figures are divided into two groups: *closed* and *not closed*. A figure that is not closed has a break in its outline, while a closed figure does not. Draw various shapes on the board, and have students classify them as "closed" or "not closed."

2. Draw a triangle and rectangle on one side of the board and a circle and semicircle on the other side. Ask students how the triangle and rectangle differ from the circle and semicircle. Help students see that the triangle and rectangle have straight sides, while the circle and semicircle have curved lines. Explain that the triangle and rectangle are *polygons* (shapes made of straight line segments). The shapes made up of curved lines are not polygons. Draw various shapes on the board, and have students classify them as "polygons" or "not polygons."

3. Give students a copy of the **Plane Figures reproducible (page 22)**. Review the categories and tell students to draw four shapes in each box, closed figures and figures that are not closed.

4. Compile students' plane figures to make class charts. Label three sheets of chart paper: *Closed Figures: Polygons; Closed Figures: Not Polygons; Figures That Are Not Closed.* Ask students to draw their figures on the appropriate charts.

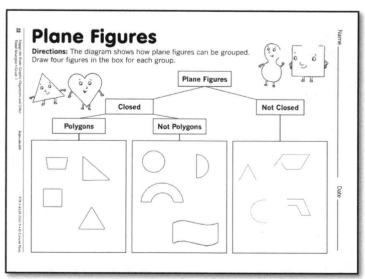

Plane Figures

Directions: The diagram shows how plane figures can be grouped. Draw four figures in the box for each group.

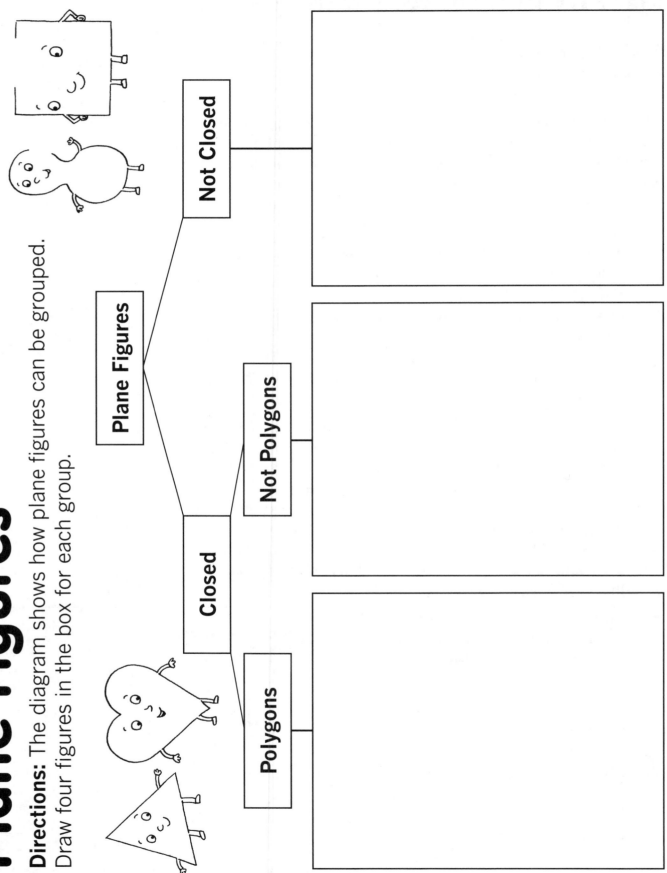

Plane Figures

Not Closed

Closed

Not Polygons

Polygons

Shape Up with Quadrilaterals: Idea Web

Skills Objectives
Recognize attributes of quadrilaterals.
Identify and classify quadrilaterals.

Materials
Quadrilateral Shapes reproducible

quadrilaterals cut from colored paper (rectangle, square, trapezoid, parallelogram, two quadrilaterals with no parallel lines, and six other shapes—at least half quadrilaterals)

tape

Geometry experiences in elementary school help develop students' spatial sense and reasoning. Younger students begin by learning shape names (e.g., square, triangle, rectangle). As their spatial reasoning develops, students start to understand why a figure is given a specific designation. For example, they can point out the square from a group of shapes as well as explain the features that make a shape a square. In third grade, students focus on a figure's specific characteristics, such as the type of lines and angles that make up the figure. In this activity, students study quadrilaterals and use an **Idea Web** to classify four-sided figures.

1. Tape the first six paper quadrilaterals to the board (rectangle, square, trapezoid, parallelogram, and two quadrilaterals with no parallel lines), and ask students how they are similar. Guide them to see that all the shapes have four sides. Explain that a polygon with four sides and four angles is called a *quadrilateral*. Write *quadrilateral* on the board. (Remind students that a *polygon* is a closed plane figure made of straight line segments. See "Plane Figures" on page 21.)

---

2. Check students' understanding of quadrilaterals by taping the next six shapes on the board. Call on volunteers to point out the shapes that are quadrilaterals.

3. Arrange the shapes so the quadrilaterals with parallel lines (rectangle, square, parallelogram, trapezoid) are on the left side of the board and those without parallel lines are on the right side. Point out that the shapes on the left have at least one pair of parallel lines, and they have special names.

4. Introduce the special quadrilaterals to the class. Label the trapezoid and ask how it differs from the other quadrilaterals with parallel lines. (The trapezoid has only one pair of parallel lines, while the other shapes have two pairs.)

5. Ask students to identify the rectangle and square, and write the shape names on the board. Then label the parallelogram. Ask students how the shapes are similar. (They have two pairs of parallel lines and their opposite sides are equal lengths.) Then ask how the shapes differ. (The rectangle and square have four right angles, but the parallelogram does not.)

6. Point to the rectangle and square. Ask how the shapes are alike and different. (Both shapes have two pairs of parallel lines and four right angles. However, only the square has all four sides of the same length.)

7. Review the names of quadrilaterals by drawing several shapes on the board. Have students identify them as rectangles, squares, trapezoids, or parallelograms.

8. As a follow-up, give students a copy of the **Quadrilateral Shapes reproducible (page 25)**. Have students read the clues in each box, write the name of the correct quadrilateral, and draw two examples. Circulate around the room to check students' work. Later, students can share and compare their answers and drawings with the class.

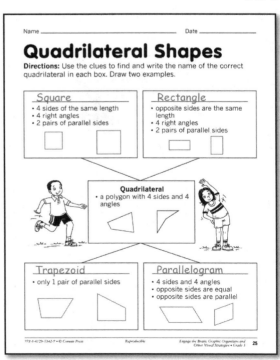

Quadrilateral Shapes

Directions: Use the clues to find and write the name of the correct quadrilateral in each box. Draw two examples.

_____

- 4 sides of the same length
- 4 right angles
- 2 pairs of parallel sides

_____

- opposite sides are the same length
- 4 right angles
- 2 pairs of parallel sides

Quadrilateral
- a polygon with 4 sides and 4 angles

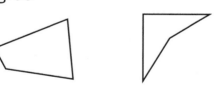

_____

- only 1 pair of parallel sides

_____

- 4 sides and 4 angles
- opposite sides are equal
- opposite sides are parallel

Exploring Area: Grid

Materials

Inch Grid reproducible

What's the Area? reproducible

transparency

3 sheets of white paper

3 different colored highlighters

tape

Skills Objectives

Understand the concept of area.
Use a grid to determine the areas of figures.
Draw figures that have a given area.

A **Grid** is a tool for measuring area, much like a ruler is a tool for measuring length. By placing the grid over the region to be measured (or by tracing the region onto the grid), students can determine the area by counting the squares. Once students are comfortable measuring shapes that fit neatly on the grid (such as rectangles), they can move on to shapes of different sizes and proportions.

1. Ahead of time, make a transparency of the **Inch Grid reproducible (page 28)**. Draw three rectangles (3" x 4", 4" x 5", and 2" x 6") on separate sheets of white paper. Use a different colored highlighter to color in each shape.

2. Tape the rectangles to the board, and ask the class to compare their sizes. Students may say that one rectangle is wider or taller than another. Explain that one way they can compare the rectangles is by measuring the area. *Area* is the number of square units that cover a region.

3. Place the transparency over the 3" x 4" rectangle. Position the Inch Grid so the rectangle fits neatly inside its squares. Ask a volunteer to count the squares in the rectangle, and write *12 square units* (or *12 square inches*) on the board. Explain that *12 square units* describes the rectangle's area because it takes 12 squares to cover the shape.

4. Call on two more volunteers, and repeat Step 3 with the remaining rectangles. Students will see that the area of the 4" x 5" rectangle is 20 square units and the area of the 2" x 6" is 12 square units. Point out that the 3" x 4" and 2" x 6" rectangles have the same area.

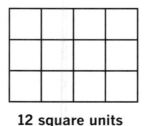

12 square units

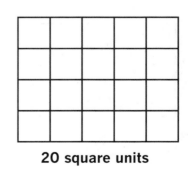

12 square units

20 square units

5. Tape a copy of the Inch Grid reproducible to the board, and draw three rectangles on it. Tell students that they can find the area of shapes by drawing them directly on the grid and counting the squares. Have them count the squares to determine the area of each rectangle.

6. Give students a copy of the Inch Grid reproducible. Tell them to draw four rectangles or squares on the grid. Then have them count the squares to determine the areas of their figures. Direct them to write the area beside each shape.

7. Finally, challenge students to find the areas of figures that only partially fit inside the grid's squares. Draw a circle on a copy of the Inch Grid reproducible, and have students count the squares to determine its area. Tell them not to count squares if they are less than half covered. Then invite students to complete the **What's the Area? reproducible (page 29)**. (Answers: heart, 4 square units; leaf, 2 square units; car, 5 square units; lamp, 5 square units; umbrella, 6 square units; arrow, 3 square units.)

Extended Learning

- Let students draw irregular figures, such as L-shapes or T-shapes, on their grids. Have them exchange papers with partners to determine the areas.

- Distribute more copies of the Inch Grid reproducible. State an area, such as *16 square units*. Have students draw on their grids a shape with the given area.

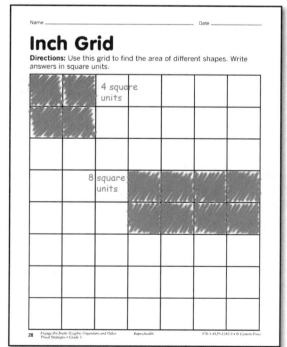

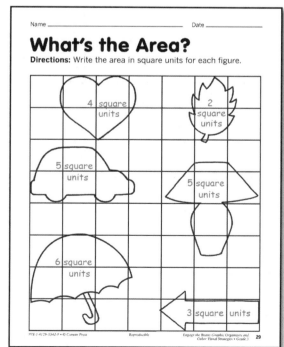

Inch Grid

Directions: Use this grid to find the area of different shapes. Write answers in square units.

Engage the Brain: Graphic Organizers and Other Visual Strategies • Grade 3   Reproducible   978-1-4129-5342-9 • © Corwin Press

What's the Area?

Directions: Write the area in square units for each figure.

Comparing Seeds: Matrix

Skills Objectives

Understand the purpose and structure of seeds.
Examine seeds for similarities and differences.

Because a **Matrix** organizes data in rows and columns, students can find information quickly and make comparisons easily. In this activity, students examine seeds and use a matrix to record their observations.

1. Show the class an apple and ask what is inside. Cut the apple in half so the seeds show. Ask students what the purpose of seeds is. Explain that plants form seeds in order to reproduce.

2. Show students an orange and an avocado. Cut them open and explain that seeds may look different, but they all have the same purpose. Seeds are made up of three parts: embryo, stored food, and seed coat.

3. Give students a copy of the **Different Kinds of Seeds reproducible (page 31)**. Then divide the class into small groups and give each group magnifying glasses, seed packets, and rulers. Tell students to examine six different seeds, draw each seed on their charts, and note the various colors. Also have them measure the seeds and record their lengths.

4. Ask students the following questions to discuss their results:
   - *How did the seeds differ?*
   - *Which seeds were the smallest? largest?*
   - *Does the color of the seed coat tell you what the color of the plant will be?*
   - *Does seed size indicate the size of the plant that will grow from it?*

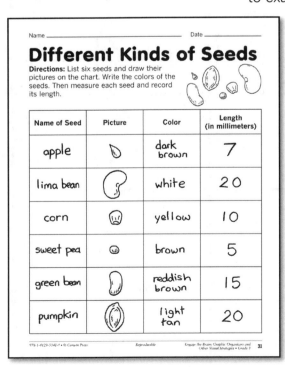

Name _____ Date _____

Different Kinds of Seeds

Directions: List six seeds and draw their pictures on the chart. Write the colors of the seeds. Then measure each seed and record its length.

Name of Seed	Picture	Color	Length (in millimeters)
apple		dark brown	7
lima bean		white	20
corn		yellow	10
sweet pea		brown	5
green bean		reddish brown	15
pumpkin		light tan	20

Name _____   Date _____

Different Kinds of Seeds

Directions: List six seeds and draw their pictures on the chart. Write the colors of the seeds. Then measure each seed and record its length.

Name of Seed	Picture	Color	Length (in millimeters)

Reproducible   *Engage the Brain: Graphic Organizers and Other Visual Strategies • Grade 3*

Animal Groups: Idea Web

Materials

Animal Groups reproducible

Five Animal Groups reproducible

pictures of animals with backbones (e.g., cat, fish, turtle)

Skills Objectives

Identify the traits of mammals, birds, fish, reptiles, and amphibians.
Give examples of mammals, birds, fish, reptiles, and amphibians.

At first, young students recognize animals by name. Later, they learn the traits that distinguish groups of animals. In this activity, students learn that vertebrates can be further classified into five main groups. They will use an **Idea Web** to display the information they've learned.

1. Tell students to touch their backs and feel the row of bones down the center. Explain that they are feeling their backbones. Many animals have backbones, too. Show pictures of some vertebrates. Tell students that vertebrates are classified into five groups.

2. Give students a copy of the **Animal Groups reproducible (page 33)**. Tell them that they will discover how vertebrates are classified.

3. Read the first paragraph aloud, and have students identify the five groups (mammals, birds, fish, reptiles, amphibians). Then call on volunteers to read the rest of the paragraphs aloud, and review the traits of each group. Discuss terms such as *warm-blooded and cold-blooded*.

4. Afterward, list the five animal groups on the board. Brainstorm animals that belong to each group and list them on the board.

5. Discuss questions such as the following to check students' understanding:
   - Which animals breathe with lungs? (mammals, birds, reptiles, adult amphibians)
   - Which animals breathe with gills? (fish, baby amphibians)
   - Which animals are cold-blooded? (fish, reptiles, amphibians)
   - Which animals feed their babies milk? (mammals)

6. As a follow-up, give students a copy of the **Five Animal Groups reproducible (page 34)**. Have them list two traits and three animals for each group. Invite students to share their answers.

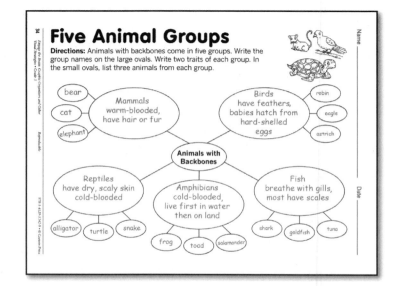

Five Animal Groups

Directions: Animals with backbones come in five groups. Write the group names on the large ovals. Write two traits of each group. In the small ovals, list three animals from each group.

bear, cat, elephant — Mammals warm-blooded, have hair or fur

Birds have feathers, babies hatch from hard-shelled eggs — robin, eagle, ostrich

Animals with Backbones

Reptiles have dry, scaly skin cold-blooded — alligator, turtle, snake

Amphibians cold-blooded, live first in water then on land — frog, toad, salamander

Fish breathe with gills, most have scales — shark, goldfish, tuna

Animal Groups

Animals with backbones are divided into five groups: mammals, birds, fish, reptiles, and amphibians.

Mammals are the only animals with hair or fur. They are warm-blooded; their body temperature stays the same even though the air temperature changes. Mammals use lungs to breathe. They give birth to live young who drink their mother's milk.

Birds are the only animals with feathers. All birds have wings and most fly. Birds are warm-blooded and breathe with lungs. Unlike mammals, babies hatch from hard-shelled eggs.

Fish live their whole lives in water. They breathe with special body parts called gills. Most fish have scales and are cold-blooded, so their body temperature changes with the temperature of the environment. Most fish lay eggs, but some give birth to live young.

Reptiles are cold-blooded animals with dry, scaly skin. They breathe with lungs. Most reptiles hatch from leathery eggs laid on land.

Amphibians are cold-blooded and have smooth skin with no scales. They live part of their lives in water and part on land. Most amphibians lay eggs in water. When the babies hatch, they live in the water and breathe with gills. Most adult amphibians live on land and breathe with lungs.

Five Animal Groups

Directions: Animals with backbones come in five groups. Write the group names on the large ovals. Write two traits of each group. In the small ovals, list three animals from each group.

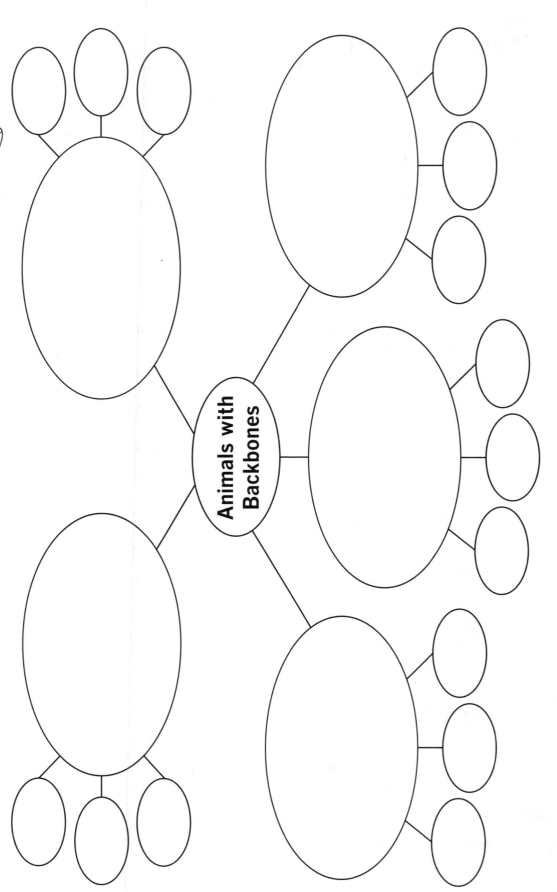

Animals with Backbones

Investigating Desert Plants: Concrete Objects

Skills Objectives
Conduct an experiment and make predictions.
Understand that living things are equipped to survive in their environment.

Materials
Desert Plants reproducible

broad-leafed houseplant (or picture)

cactus (or picture)

paper towels

bowl of water

Science involves experimentation and discovery. When planning your science lessons, include hands-on explorations using **Concrete Objects** that encourage students to investigate scientific concepts, make careful observations, and draw reasonable conclusions. In this activity, students conduct a simple experiment to learn how desert plants are specially suited for their harsh, dry environment.

1. Show students a broad-leafed houseplant and a cactus. Point out that the houseplant has broad, flat leaves while the cactus has none. Explain that most cacti live in dry, desert regions. Tell students they will perform a simple experiment to see why cacti and other desert plants do not need broad, flat leaves in order to survive.

2. Give students a copy of the **Desert Plants reproducible (page 36)**. Divide the class into groups of two or three, and give each group two paper towels and a bowl of water.

3. Have students read the question at the top of the page and then predict an answer. Instruct them to write their prediction on the lines.

4. Read Steps 1–3 together and have students conduct the experiment. (They will dampen two paper towels, laying one out flat and rolling up the other. Students will place the paper towels in a sunny location for one hour.)

5. Let students check the paper towels after an hour and record their observations. (They will find that the flat paper towel is drier than the rolled-up paper towel.)

6. Discuss results with the class. Ask why desert plants don't have broad, flat leaves. Guide students to see that broad, flat leaves would cause cacti to lose water quickly. Explain that most desert plants have either very small leaves or none at all. Discuss the various ways cacti are able to store water to survive.

Desert Plants

Directions: Read the question and write a prediction. Then follow the steps to do an experiment that will test your prediction.

Question:

Why do you think desert plants don't have broad, flat leaves? Write your prediction.

_____

_____

Do an Experiment:

1. Fold two paper towels into fourths. Dip each towel into a bowl of water. Squeeze out the excess water.
2. Unfold the paper towels. Lay out one towel so it lies flat. Roll up the other towel.
3. Place the paper towels in a sunny place. Check on the towels after one hour.

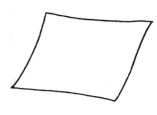

Results:

How did the paper towels look and feel?

Flat paper towel: _____

Rolled paper towel: _____

Conclusion:

Why don't desert plants have broad, flat leaves?

_____

_____

Changes in Matter: T-Chart

Skills Objectives
Recognize changes in matter.
Distinguish between physical changes and chemical changes.

Materials
Changes in Matter reproducible

banana

knife and cutting board

ice cube

1/2 cup vinegar

1 tablespoon baking soda

clear glass

raw and hard-boiled egg

small bowl

Matter is constantly changing. Some changes are physical (in which the substance stays the same). Other changes are chemical (in which particles of matter change to form new kinds of matter). In this activity, students investigate changes in matter and organize the data on a **T-Chart** to indicate whether the changes are physical or chemical. A T-chart allows students to readily see what qualifies as a physical change and what qualifies as a chemical change.

1. Show a banana to students and slice it into several pieces. Ask how the banana changed. (*It got smaller; it was split into pieces.*) Ask if the banana itself is still a banana. Help students see that the banana is still the same substance it was before it was cut. Explain that cutting the banana is an example of a *physical change.*

2. Show an ice cube to the class. Ask if water freezing into ice is an example of a physical change or a chemical change. Explain that the state of matter changes when water freezes (liquid turns to solid) but the change is still physical. The ice is still the same substance as liquid water.

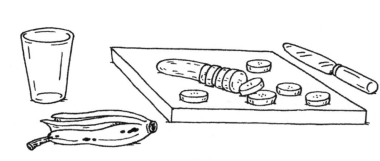

3. Next, pour ½ cup of vinegar into a clear glass. Add 1 tablespoon of baking soda to the glass. The mixture will start to fizz. Explain that the fizzing occurs because a gas called carbon dioxide is being produced. Mixing vinegar with baking soda results in a *chemical change.* During a chemical change, the particles in the original matter change, and new matter is formed.

4. Show students a raw egg and a peeled boiled egg. Crack the raw egg into a bowl and display the yolk and egg white. Explain that boiling an egg results in a chemical change. Point out the difference in appearance between the uncooked egg and the boiled egg. When food is cooked, a chemical change takes place and the original substance is altered.

5. Give students a copy of the **Changes in Matter reproducible (page 39)**. Then write the following phrases on the board. Have students list each one on their papers as a physical change or a chemical change. (Answers are in parentheses.)
   - paper gets folded (physical)
   - ice melts to liquid (physical)
   - wood is burned (chemical)
   - bread gets moldy (chemical)
   - a nail gets rusty (chemical)
   - fabric gets torn (physical)
   - gasoline is burned (chemical)
   - leaves turn color in fall (chemical)
   - peanuts and raisins are mixed in a bowl (physical)
   - a slice of apple turns brown (chemical)
   - salt is mixed with water (physical)
   - milk turns sour (chemical)
   - a chair gets painted (physical)
   - clothes get wet (physical)

6. Invite students to compare their answers with a partner. Then have partners discuss several things they do during the day that result in a physical change or a chemical change (e.g., brush teeth, physical; make toast, chemical).

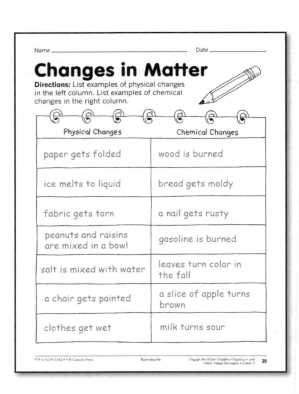

Changes in Matter

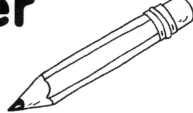

Directions: List examples of physical changes in the left column. List examples of chemical changes in the right column.

Physical Changes	Chemical Changes

Heat Changes Food: Wheel Organizer

Skills Objectives

Recognize that heat is an important part of food preparation.
Understand that heat affects food in different ways.

Third graders are familiar with heat, light, and other forms of energy. Although they may not fully understand energy in scientific terms, students have observed its applications, such as cooking food and turning on lights, in everyday life. In this activity, students explore the effect of heat on food. Then they use a **Wheel Organizer** to organize and record their results.

1. Show students a slice of bread and ask them to describe how it looks and feels. Ask what will happen to the bread when you put it in the toaster, and then toast the bread. Point out that the bread becomes brown and crisp. Explain that heat affects foods in different ways. Bread, for example, gets harder when heated.

2. Invite students to think about the foods they eat and name foods that harden when cooked or heated (e.g., *eggs, meat, pancakes*).

3. Place a piece of chocolate on a plate, and leave it in a sunny location. Ask students to predict what will happen to the chocolate. After several minutes, check the chocolate. Students will see that the chocolate melts in the heat. Ask them to suggest other foods that melt when heated (e.g., *ice cream, cheese, butter*).

4. Hold up a potato. Stab the potato with a fork to show how hard it is. Then ask students what happens when a potato is cooked. (*It gets softer.*) Have them name other foods that get softer when heated (e.g., *carrots, rice, macaroni*).

5. Give students a copy of the **Heat and Food reproducible (page 41)**. Ask them to list at least four examples for each section of the cooking pan. As students work, check that they are completing their organizers correctly.

6. Compile students' responses to make a class chart that presents how heat changes food.

Heat and Food

Directions: List foods in each section of the pan to show how they change when heated.

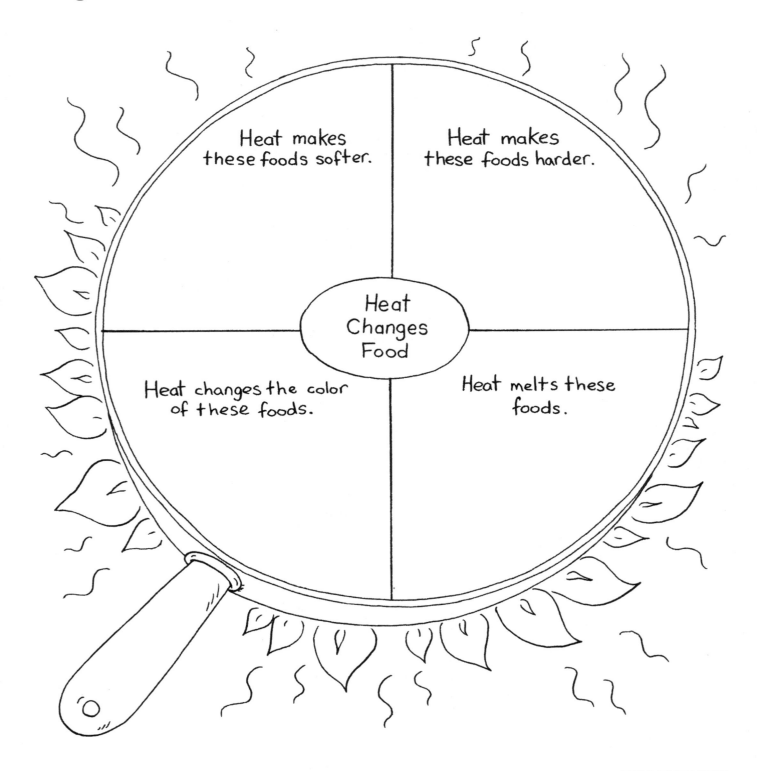

Heat makes these foods softer.

Heat makes these foods harder.

Heat Changes Food

Heat changes the color of these foods.

Heat melts these foods.

Layers of the Earth: Model and Diagram

Materials

Layers of the Earth reproducible

apple

globe

knife and cutting board

chart paper

Skills Objectives

Read for information.

Recognize the earth's three layers.

Label a diagram.

Models and **Diagrams** are helpful for introducing scientific concepts, including topics such as the structure of the earth. Since we cannot drill into the earth and take pictures of its interior, models and diagrams provide visuals that help students understand the concept.

1. Display an apple and a globe, and ask what the two items have in common. Tell students that both the apple and the earth are made up of layers.

2. Cut the apple in half, and hold up one of the halves. Point to the apple's skin, and explain that a thin layer covers the entire apple. Similarly, a thin layer of solid rock covers the earth. This layer of rock is called the *crust*; it forms the dry land and the ocean floors.

3. Next, point to the apple's flesh that lies just below the skin. The flesh is the thickest layer. Explain that the *mantle*, which lies below the crust, is the thickest layer of the earth.

4. Point to the center of the apple. Tell students that the earth also has a center; it is called the *core*. The core is divided into two parts: the outer core of liquid rock and the inner core of solid metal.

5. Give each student a copy of the **Layers of the Earth reproducible (page 43)**. Point to the diagram of the earth, and ask students to identify the earth's three layers. Have them read the passage and fill in the chart to show what they learned about the earth's crust, mantle, and core.

6. Let students share their responses with the class. Compile their responses on a large sheet of chart paper to make a class chart.

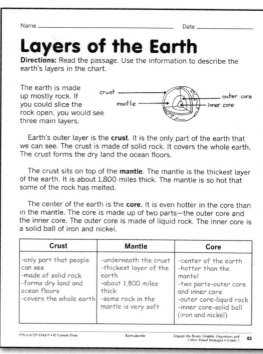

Layers of the Earth

Directions: Read the passage. Use the information to describe the earth's layers in the chart.

The earth is made up mostly rock. If you could slice the rock open, you would see three main layers.

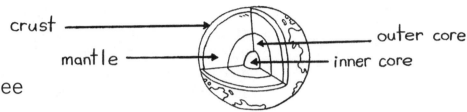

Earth's outer layer is the **crust**. It is the only part of the earth that we can see. The crust is made of solid rock. It covers the whole earth. The crust forms the dry land the ocean floors.

The crust sits on top of the **mantle**. The mantle is the thickest layer of the earth. It is about 1,800 miles thick. The mantle is so hot that some of the rock has melted.

The center of the earth is the **core**. It is even hotter in the core than in the mantle. The core is made up of two parts—the outer core and the inner core. The outer core is made of liquid rock. The inner core is a solid ball of iron and nickel.

Crust	Mantle	Core

Shadow Lengths: Graph

Materials

paper plates

pencils

Skills Objectives

Observe and record changes.

Draw conclusions based on observations.

Understand how the sun's position in the sky affects shadows.

A **Graph** presents data in a visual form that makes comparing items easier. In this activity, students make a simple sundial that records how shadows lengthen or shorten during the day. The sundial is actually a graph that displays different shadow lengths. By analyzing the data, students can draw conclusions about how the sun's position in the sky affects shadows.

1. Take students outside early on a sunny day. Invite them to look at their shadows, and discuss what causes them. Explain that when they stand in the sunlight, their bodies block some of the light and create shadows on the ground.

2. Tell students that they will be conducting an experiment to observe what happens to shadows during the day. Then divide the class into small groups and give each group a paper plate and two pencils.

3. Take students to a grassy spot and instruct them to poke a pencil through the center of their paper plate. Show them how to push the pencil into the ground so the plate lies flat and the pencil stands upright.

4. Point out the pencil's shadow on the plate. Instruct students to use their other pencil to make a line around the shadow. Have students write the time on the line.

5. Take students outside every hour to mark the shadow lines. Continue throughout the day until they have drawn four or five lines on their plates.

6. Have students bring their plates indoors. Initiate a discussion about the results by asking the following questions:

- *How did the shadows change during the day?* (Their lengths changed. Also, the shadows moved from one side of the plate to the other.)
- *When were the shadows the shortest?* (about noon)
- *When were the shadows the longest?* (early in the morning and later in the day)
- *How would the sundial look if the class had started an hour earlier and ended an hour later?* (The pencil line at each end of the plate would be longer.)

7. Help students see that the sun's position in the sky affects the lengths of shadows. Explain that the pencil's shadow was the shortest around noon, when the sun was high in the sky. The shadow was the longest in the early morning and late afternoon, when the sun was low in the sky. The shadows moved around the plate as the sun moved. Tell students that shadows fall westward as the sun rises in the east; later in the day, shadows fall eastward as the sun starts to set in the west.

Extended Learning

Show a picture of a sundial to the class. Tell students that people long ago used sundials to tell time. Shadows lengthened or shortened as they moved around the dial, and people could approximate the time of day.

Amazing Planets: Venn Diagram

Materials

Comparing Two Planets reproducible

picture of planets in the solar system

library books, magazines, and other references about planets

Skills Objectives

Research key facts.
Distinguish similarities and differences.

A **Venn Diagram** is a useful tool for making comparisons because it allows students to easily organize and record similarities and differences. In this activity, students research two planets and make a Venn diagram showing how the planets are alike and different.

1. Display a picture that shows all the planets lined up in order by their distances from the sun. Discuss how the planets are alike and different. Students may suggest that all the planets are round and move in space. However, planets differ greatly in size and in their distance from the sun.

2. Give students library books and other references so they can choose two planets to compare. As students research their planets, have them list important facts. Write prompts on the board, such as: *How large is the planet? How far away is it from the sun? Does it have a moon? What does its surface look like?*

3. When students are done with their research, give them a copy of the **Comparing Two Planets reproducible (page 47)**. Tell students they will use their facts to write words and phrases in the Venn diagram.

4. Model an example by drawing two large, overlapping circles on the board. Write *Earth* over one circle and *Mercury* over the other. Have students suggest one way the two planets differ (e.g., *Earth has a blanket of air surrounding it, but Mercury has almost no atmosphere*). Write differences on the outer parts of the circles. Then ask how the planets are similar (e.g., *They both orbit the sun*). Write similarities in the overlapping part of the diagram.

5. Check students' work as they complete their diagrams. When they're finished, work as a class to make a *Planets in Our Solar System* bulletin board display. Invite students to offer information from their Venn diagrams to illustrate and list facts about each planet.

Comparing Two Planets

Directions: Compare two planets. Write their names at the tops of the circles. Write how the planets are different in the outer parts of the circles and how they are like alike in the overlapping part.

Mercury
Planet

-diameter of about 3,000 miles
-length of year is 88 Earth days
-length of day is 59 Earth days
-almost no atmosphere
-surface has many craters
-planet closest to the sun
-moves around the sun faster than any other planet

-round
-orbits the sun
-one of the "inner planets"
-no moons

Venus
Planet

-diameter of about 7,500 miles
-length of year is 225 Earth days
-length of day is 243 Earth days
-dense atmosphere
-covered by thick, yellowish clouds
-has huge volcanoes

Name

Date

Comparing Two Planets

Directions: Compare two planets. Write their names at the tops of the circles. Write how the planets are different in the outer parts of the circles and how they are like alike in the overlapping part.

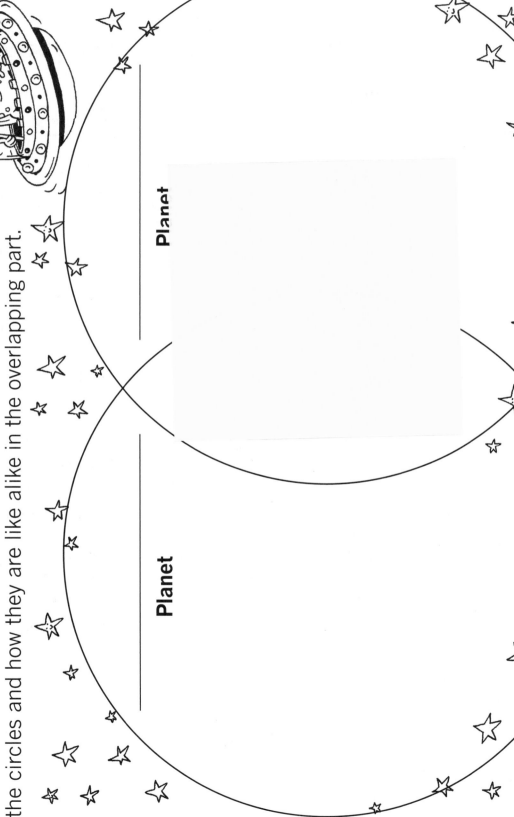

Planet

Planet

CHAPTER 3

Social Studies

Building Communities: Sequence Chart

Materials

Choosing a Place to Live reproducible

The Pilgrims of Plimoth by Marcia Sewall

Skills Objectives

Recognize that geographical features influence where communities are built. Write steps of a process in sequential order.

A **Sequence Chart** presents a series of events in order. In this activity, students make a sequence chart showing how they would decide where to build a successful community.

1. Hold up the book *The Pilgrims of Plimoth*. Explain that it describes the Pilgrims' early days in America. Then read aloud pages 6–12.

2. Discuss the first place the Pilgrims landed. Turn to page 8 and ask what "the land offered nothing" means. Explain that the area was not a suitable place to start a settlement. It was dangerous, and there were no resources like food and lumber.

3. Discuss where the Pilgrims finally settled. Have students explain why this area was better.

4. Ask students: *Did people long ago just pick any place to start a community?* Elicit from students that several factors influenced people's decisions about where to live. Brainstorm and write factors on the board: climate, water, crops, wood.

5. Give students a copy of the **Choosing a Place to Live reproducible (page 49)**. Tell them to imagine they are starting a community in an unsettled area. Have students write the factors they would consider and arrange them in order of importance.

6. Afterward, invite groups to discuss their ideas and present a list to the class.

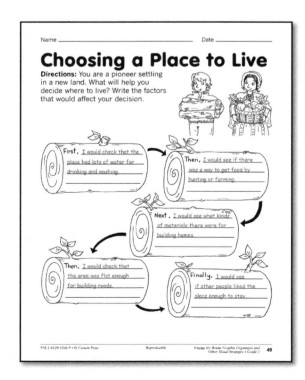

Name _____ Date _____

Choosing a Place to Live

Directions: You are a pioneer settling in a new land. What will help you decide where to live? Write the factors that would affect your decision.

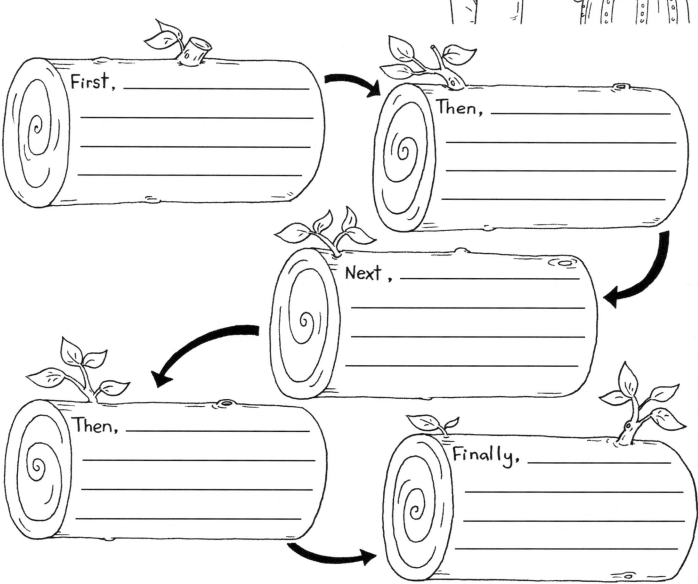

First, _____
_____
_____
_____

Then, _____
_____
_____
_____

Next, _____
_____
_____
_____

Then, _____
_____
_____
_____

Finally, _____
_____
_____
_____

Communities Change: Photos and T-Chart

Materials

Communities Change reproducible

early photos of your community (check the local library, historical society, or Internet)

current photos or brochures of your community

chart paper

Skills Objectives

Make observations.

Recognize how various factors influence communities' growth.

In this activity, students look at early photos of their community to see how the area has changed. **Photos** allow students to directly observe how their community's size and appearance has been altered by growth. Students then record their observations on a **T-Chart**.

1. Display early photos of your community. Discuss where and when the photos were taken. Ask students if they recognize the locations.

2. Show students some current photos of your community. Talk about how your community has grown and changed over the years. Discuss reasons for the changes. (As businesses and industries grew, new jobs were created and more people came to live in the area. As more people came, more homes and stores were built.)

3. Post the photos in various places around the room, and give students a copy of the **Communities Change reproducible (page 51)**.

4. Divide the class into small groups. Have groups view all the photos and list words or phrases that describe them on their reproducibles. Guide students with questions such as: *What do the roads look like? What forms of transportation do you see? Are there wide, open spaces? What do the buildings look like?*

5. Invite each group to share their observations and compile their findings on a class chart. Help students see that the photos reveal not only how the community changed in size and appearance but also the way people lived and worked.

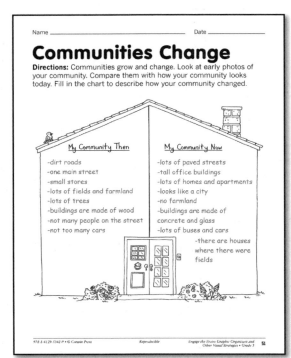

Name _____   Date _____

Communities Change

Directions: Communities grow and change. Look at early photos of your community. Compare them with how your community looks today. Fill in the chart to describe how your community changed.

My Community Then

My Community Now

Superstores! Lists

Materials

Stores in My Community reproducible

bag of groceries

bag of new clothes (e.g., pair of socks, shirt, scarf)

several copies of the local phone book

newspapers and store flyers

Skills Objectives

Recognize that stores provide an important service.

Skim for information.

Match stores and products.

This activity presents students with **Lists** of products their families might buy. Students will learn that many types of stores are needed to provide for people's needs.

1. Display a bag of groceries. Ask students where you bought the items. Then show a bag of new clothes. Ask where you bought these items. Guide students to see that people in a community need many products.

2. Give students a copy of the **Stores in My Community reproducible (page 53)**. Then divide the class into small groups and provide each group with newspaper ads, store flyers, and a phone book.

3. Point to the first shopping list. Ask what kind of store sells these items. Write *grocery store* or *supermarket* on the board. Invite students to name a list of stores that sell groceries. Have each student choose a name to write on his or her paper.

4. Repeat Step 3 with the second list. If students do not know the names of specific sports stores, let them look through the phone book or store flyers.

5. Tell groups to complete the page. Later, invite them to share how they know of specific stores.

Extended Learning

Divide the class into nine groups, and assign each group one of the following stores: grocery store, sports store, clothing store, toy store, bookstore, drugstore, pet store, bakery, furniture store. Have students make a poster highlighting or advertising the different stores in their category.

Name _____ Date _____

Stores in My Community

Directions: Stores provide products that people need. Look at each shopping list and write the name of a store where you can buy the products. Use the phone book or newspaper ads to help you.

milk eggs apples	baseball mitt running shoes tennis racket	jeans shirt coat
1. A-1 Market	2. Super Sports	3. Coat Maker
balloons yo-yo puzzle	magazine dictionary storybooks	vitamins medicine cough drops
4. OK Toy Store	5. Leah's Books	6. ABC Drugstore
dog food fish tank bird cage	bread birthday cake cookies	bed table chair
7. Petmania	8. Big's Bakery	9. Furniture Town

978-1-4129-5342-9 • © Corwin Press   Reproducible   *Engage the Brain: Graphic Organizers and Other Visual Strategies • Grade 3*   **53**

Stores in My Community

Directions: Stores provide products that people need. Look at each shopping list and write the name of a store where you can buy the products. Use the phone book or newspaper ads to help you.

1. _____

2. _____

3. _____

4. _____

5. _____

6. _____

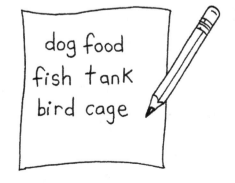

7. _____

8. _____

9. _____

Native Americans: Sectioned Chart

Materials

Native American Group reproducible

pictures of Native Americans from different regions

Skills Objectives

Research a topic and identify key facts.
Understand that cultures are shaped by environment.

Native Americans were the first people to live in the Americas. The various groups differed greatly in their languages, traditions, and ways of life. In this activity, students research a Native American group and summarize key points on a **Sectioned Chart**.

1. Write the following words on the board: *canoe, kayak, moccasin,* and *toboggan*. Ask students: *What do these words mean? What do they have in common?* Explain that Native Americans invented these words.

2. Tell students that Native Americans lived in North America thousands of years before anyone else did. Display pictures of Native American groups from different regions. Guide students to realize that many tribes made up the different groups, and each group had a distinct way of life.

3. Instruct students to research a Native American group, such as the Plains Indians. (If you wish, let them choose a specific tribe, such as the Sioux.) Give students a copy of the **Native American Group reproducible (page 55)**, and tell them to research each topic and write words or phrases showing their findings.

4. As students work, walk around the room and check that their notes adequately communicate key facts and ideas.

5. When students are finished, have them find or draw pictures to complement their charts. They can share their illustrated charts in small groups.

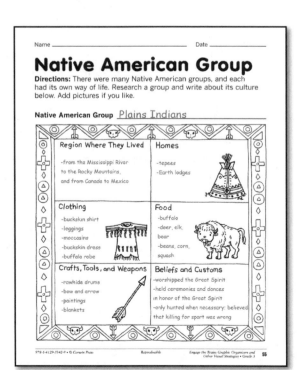

Native American Group

Directions: There were many Native American groups, and each had its own way of life. Research a group and write about its culture below. Add pictures if you like.

Native American Group _____

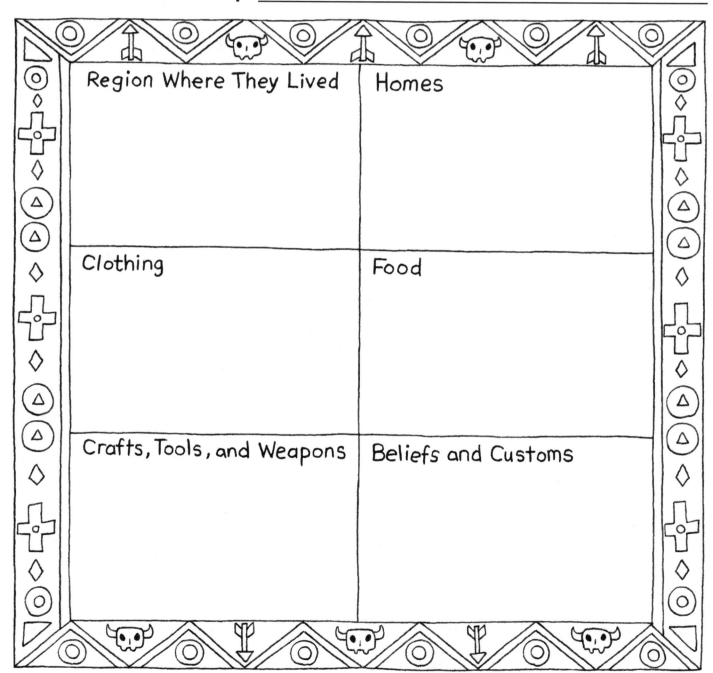

Region Where They Lived	Homes
Clothing	Food
Crafts, Tools, and Weapons	Beliefs and Customs

A Nation of Immigrants: World Map

Materials

World Map reproducible

chart paper

wall world map

sticky notes

Skills Objectives

Identify various groups of people who immigrated to the United States.
Recognize that many cultures contributed to America's growth.
Identify the different countries represented by students.

The United States has one of the world's most varied populations. In fact, it has been called a "nation of immigrants." From the 1820s to 1920s, millions of immigrants came to America. In this activity, students research their family backgrounds and discover where their families originated. They then mark those places on a **World Map**. A map not only highlights various countries but also allows students see how far people traveled to start a new life in a foreign land.

1. Tell students to stand. Ask the following questions, one at a time. For each question, students who answer *no* must sit down while the rest remain standing.
   - *Were you born in the United States?*
   - *Were your parents born in the United States?*
   - *Were your grandparents born in the United States?*
   - *Did your family have its beginnings in North America?*

2. Afterward, most or all students should be sitting down. Explain that most or all of the students in the room have family members who came to North America from another place. Explain that the Native Americans were the first people to inhabit the Americas, but even they came from another land. (Native Americans traveled from Asia to the Americas thousands of years ago.)

3. Tell students that the United States has been called a "nation of immigrants" because so much of its population is made up of people from different lands. For homework, have students find the names of the countries where their families originated. Instruct them to write down the information and bring it back to school.

4. The next day, make a chart listing students' names and their corresponding countries of origin. As students study the chart, have them note if some countries appear more than others. Make a tally chart showing the different countries represented by students in your classroom.

Student	Country
Ricky	Korea
Michael	France, England
Nikki	Australia
Brian	England
Karina	Mexico
Emilio	Mexico

5. Display a large world map and give students a copy of the **World Map reproducible (page 58)**. Read the names of students' countries one by one, and use a sticky note to mark their locations on the map. Invite students to find the approximate locations on their reproducible map, and color a dot on each place.

6. After all the countries are marked, have students refer to their maps to discuss the following questions:
   - *How many different countries are represented in the class?*
   - *From which country are most of our families?*
   - *Many families traveled to North America by boat. Which families do you think came across the Pacific? Which families do you think came across the Atlantic?*

Extended Learning

Share Ellen Levine's *If Your Name Was Changed at Ellis Island* with the class. This book vividly describes what happened to immigrants who entered the United States through Ellis Island, an immigration center in New York Harbor.

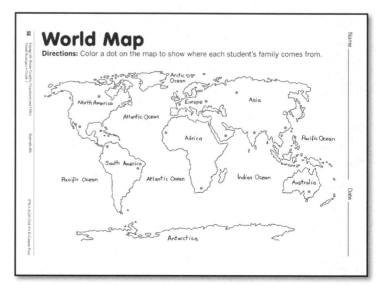

World Map

Directions: Color a dot on the map to show where each student's family comes from.

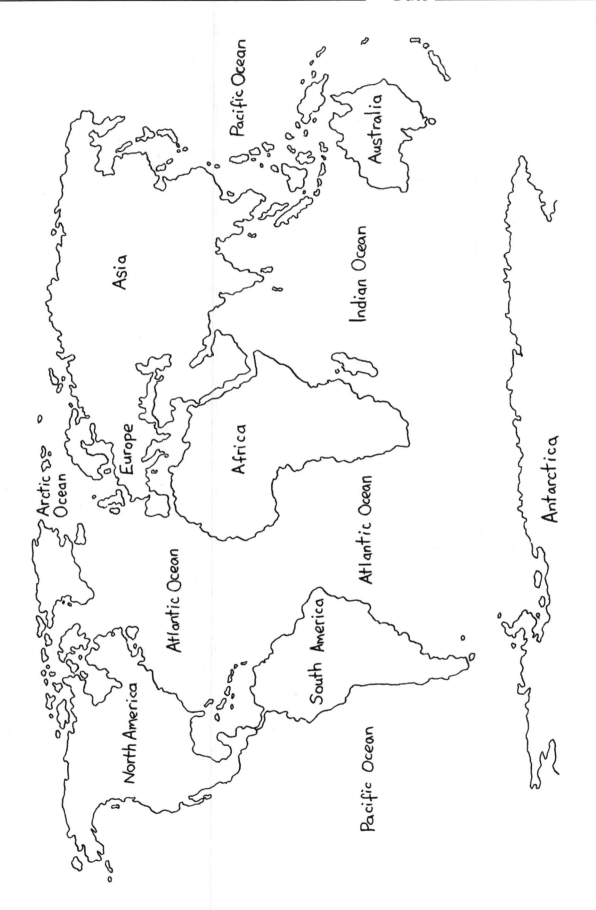

Arctic Ocean

Asia

Pacific Ocean

Australia

Europe

Indian Ocean

Africa

Atlantic Ocean

North America

Atlantic Ocean

South America

Antarctica

Pacific Ocean

 Engage the Brain: Graphic Organizers and Other Visual Strategies • Grade 3 Reproducible *978-1-4129-5342-9 • © Corwin Press*

Our Basic Needs: Poster

Skills Objectives
Recognize that all people have the same needs.
Research information.
Communicate key facts.

Materials
library books, encyclopedias, and other references about families and societies around the world

poster board

art supplies

People all over the world share the same basic needs. Physical needs include food and protection from the elements. Emotional needs include love and a sense of belonging. In this activity, students explore how basic needs are met in countries around the world. They then summarize what they learned by making a **Poster**.

1. Show pictures of families from different countries. Ask how the families are different (e.g., *They wear different clothing and live in different kinds of homes*). Then ask how the families are similar (e.g., *They eat meals together. Family members care for each other*).

2. Tell students that all people share basic needs no matter where they live. Every human being needs food, clothing, and shelter. Discuss why these needs are called "basic." (People can't survive unless those needs are met.) Explain that other needs are also considered basic, such as love, safety, and a sense of belonging.

3. Set out library books, encyclopedias, and other references that show how people live in various countries. Then pair up students and have each pair choose a country. Over several days, let students research how basic needs are met in the country they chose. Tell them to take notes on their research. Check students' notes periodically to make sure they understand the task.

4. After research is completed, have partners make posters showing what they learned. Posters should be titled with the country's name and display pictures and text that demonstrate how basic needs are met.

5. Display posters around the classroom. Initiate a discussion to review how different cultures and societies around the world meet people's needs in similar ways.

Inventions Change Lives: Timeline

Materials

Inventions Timeline reproducible

library books, encyclopedias, and other references about inventions

can opener, flashlight, toaster (or pictures)

butcher paper (optional)

Skills Objectives

Understand the impact of inventions on people's lives.

Identify important inventions.

Arrange events in chronological order.

Inventions, such as cars, electric light, and personal computers have transformed the way we live. In this activity, students create a **Timeline** that features the inventions they consider important.

1. Show students a can opener, a flashlight, and a toaster. Discuss the purpose of each item and ask how it helps people. Explain that many inventions make our lives easier. Then brainstorm with students some inventions they have at home and list them on the board.

2. Point out one of the items you listed. Discuss how life would be different if that item had not been invented. For example, if no one had invented the washing machine, people would still be washing clothes by hand.

3. Provide library books, encyclopedias, and other references about inventions. Ask students to choose five inventions that have greatly affected the way people live. Have them list the inventions and the years they were invented.

4. Give students a copy of the **Inventions Timeline reproducible (page 61)**. Point out the five blank boxes along the horizontal line. Have students write the years of invention in order in these boxes.

5. Next, point out the large boxes. Tell students to complete their timelines by filling in these boxes with facts about their inventions.

6. Afterward, invite students to share their timelines. Compile the information from students' timelines onto one large timeline drawn on butcher paper.

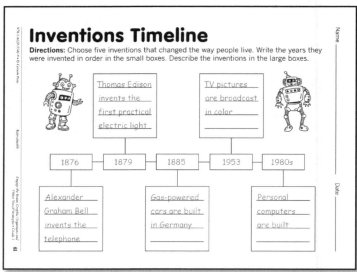

Inventions Timeline

Directions: Choose five inventions that changed the way people live. Write the years they were invented in order in the small boxes. Describe the inventions in the large boxes.

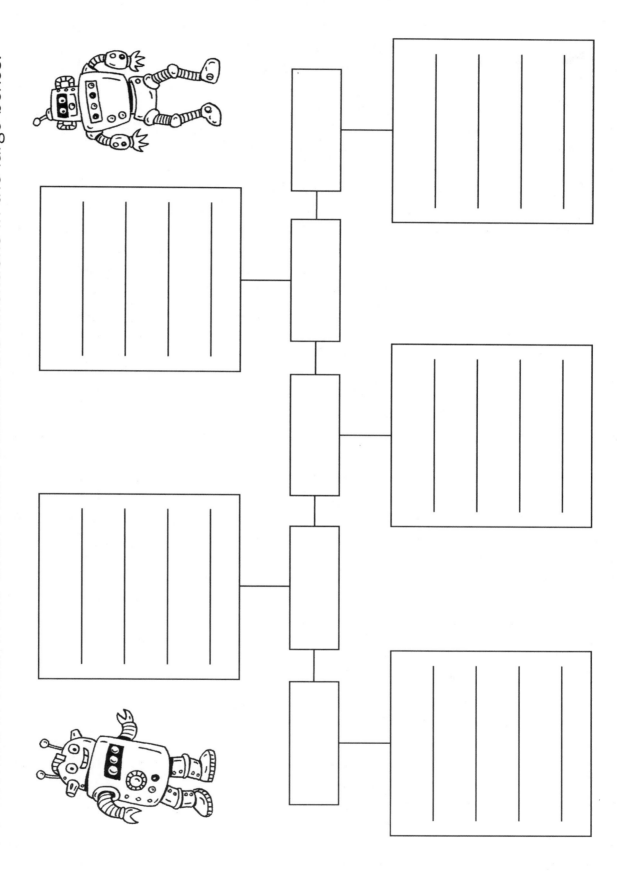

New State Flag: Diagram

Materials

New State Flag reproducible

United States flag (or picture)

your state flag (or picture)

crayons or markers

Skills Objectives

Research information.

Identify main ideas.

Design symbols to convey concepts.

The symbols on each U.S. state flag reflects the state's characteristics, such as history and geography. In this activity, students design a flag presenting their state's most noteworthy qualities. The completed flag is a **Diagram** that "maps out" the state's identity.

1. Point to the U.S. flag. Ask students what the colors and symbols mean. Explain that the 13 stripes stand for the original 13 colonies. The 50 stars stand for the 50 U.S. states. The red means courage; the white, purity; and the blue, justice.

2. Show a picture of your state flag. Explain that this flag represents those things that make your state stand out from the other states. Identify the meanings of the flag's symbols.

3. Ask students what the U.S. flag and state flags have in common. Explain that both incorporate symbols of unique qualities.

4. Give students a copy of the **New State Flag reproducible (page 63)**. Then tell them to imagine they've been hired to design a new state flag. Ask what they would feature. Write their ideas on the board.

5. Invite students to draw symbols on their flag that represent unique characteristics of their state. When flags are decorated, have students write the meaning of each symbol.

6. Afterward, invite students to explain their flags' symbols for the class. Arrange the flags around the classroom for a colorful display.

New State Flag

Directions: Design a new flag for your state. On a separate sheet of paper, explain the meanings of the symbols you used.

CHAPTER 4

Language Arts

What Makes a Story? Story Web

Materials

Spin a Story
reproducible

Miss Rumphius by
Barbara Cooney

Skills Objectives

Recognize story elements.

Identify the story elements of a particular story.

All stories contain the following elements: setting, main character(s), problem, and solution. A **Story Web** helps students analyze a story and identify each element. Mapping out the information on a web lets students see how the writer combines individual elements to create an intriguing story.

1. Display the book *Miss Rumphius* for the class. Ask students what they think the book is about. Then read it aloud. (The story tells of a girl who sets out to achieve three goals: travel to distant places, live by the sea, and make the world more beautiful. She achieves all but the last goal. When Miss Rumphius sees lupines growing on a hillside and realizes the wind blew the seeds there from her garden, she knows what to do. From then on, every summer she scatters lupine seeds around the countryside so they will cover the hills in spring.)

2. After reading the story, give students a copy of the **Spin a Story reproducible (page 66)**. Copy the story web on the board for students.

Write the title and author on your web, and have students do the same on their papers.

3. Read the headings on the four outer boxes of the web. Explain that every story is made up of the same basic elements. The *setting* sets the stage for the story; it tells when and where the story takes place. One or more *main characters* provide the focal point of the story; events in the story revolve around them. Every story also has a *problem*—something that needs to be resolved before the story ends. The *solution* and its aftermath bring an end to the story.

4. Discuss the setting of *Miss Rumphius*. (The story is set in America about 100 years ago.) Then have students write the setting in the appropriate box on their webs. Write the information on your web as well.

5. Ask students to identify the main character (Miss Rumphius). Have them add her name to their webs while you do the same.

6. Discuss the problem in the story. Talk about Miss Rumphius reaching her first two goals. Ask students why she wasn't satisfied. (She still had one goal left.) Then have students work with you to write a summary of the problem on their webs.

7. Finally, talk about how Miss Rumphius solved her problem. She decides that she will scatter lupine seeds every summer to make the countryside beautiful. Help students write a summary of the solution on their webs.

8. Afterward, have students look at the webs they created. Tell them that the web displays the basic framework of *Miss Rumphius*: setting, main character, problem, and solution. Remind students that every story has these elements.

9. Use the story web to analyze other stories with students. Or, allow students to take home story webs and use them to analyze a story they are reading on their own.

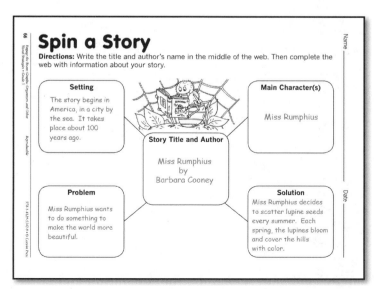

Spin a Story

Directions: Write the title and author's name in the middle of the web. Then complete the web with information about your story.

Name _____

Setting
The story begins in America, in a city by the sea. It takes place about 100 years ago.

Main Character(s)
Miss Rumphius

Story Title and Author
Miss Rumphius
by
Barbara Cooney

Problem
Miss Rumphius wants to do something to make the world more beautiful.

Solution
Miss Rumphius decides to scatter lupine seeds every summer. Each spring, the lupines bloom and cover the hills with color.

Date _____

Name _____ Date _____

Spin a Story

Directions: Write the title and author's name in the middle of the web. Then complete the web with information about your story.

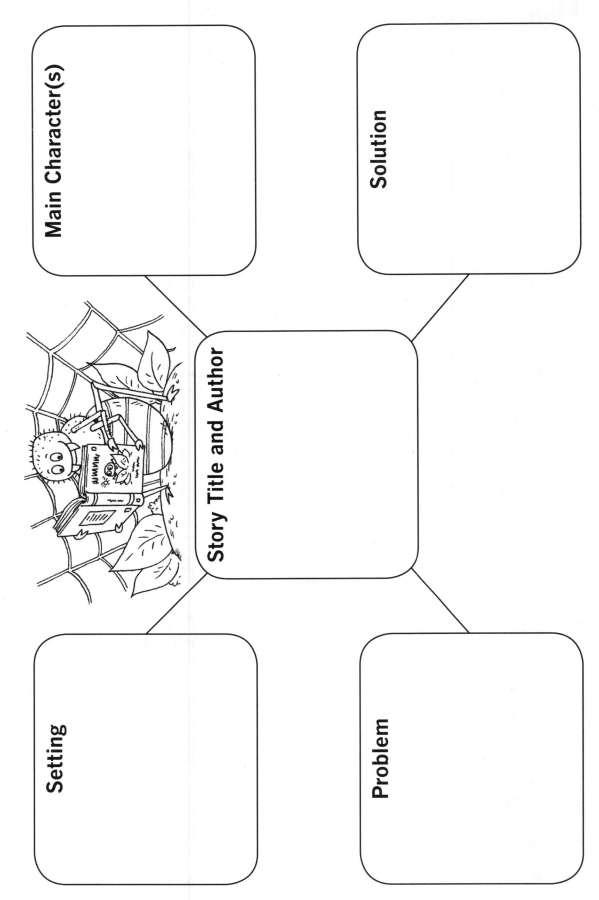

Main Character(s)

Solution

Story Title and Author

Setting

Problem

Engage the Brain: Graphic Organizers and Other Visual Strategies • Grade 3   Reproducible   978-1-4129-5342-9 • © Corwin Press

Plan a Story: Story Web

Skills Objectives
Identify story elements.
Plan an outline for a story.
Write a story based on an outline.

Materials
Spin a Story
reproducible

Miss Rumphius by
Barbara Cooney

A **Story Web** is an excellent tool for helping students plan and organize ideas for their own stories. Begin by having students identify the elements in a familiar story. Using that story's structure as a model, students can plan their own tales. This activity is based on the book *Miss Rumphius* (see "What Makes a Story?" on pages 64–65), but any familiar book may be used.

1. Review *Miss Rumphius* by having students identify its setting, main characters, problem, and solution. Remind the class that all stories contain these elements.

2. Discuss Miss Rumphius' goal to beautify the world. Then have students imagine they are going to rewrite the story. Invite them to think of a goal the main character might have. The goal may be realistic (wanting to help others) or imaginary (wanting special powers). Brainstorm ideas and list them on the board. Also discuss how the character might achieve his or her goals.

3. Give students a copy of the **Spin a Story reproducible (page 66)**. Instruct them to create the framework for their stories by writing the setting, main characters, problem, and solution on the web. They can refer to the ideas on the board. If you wish, let students work in pairs or small groups so they can continue brainstorming. Check that students are using their webs correctly.

4. Invite students to write their stories. As they work on their drafts, check that they are developing their stories in a logical, cohesive manner. Students will also need to check their work for mechanics such as punctuation, grammar, and spelling. Writing may take several days.

5. When the stories are completed, ask students to share them in small groups. Afterward, bind stories into a book for your classroom library.

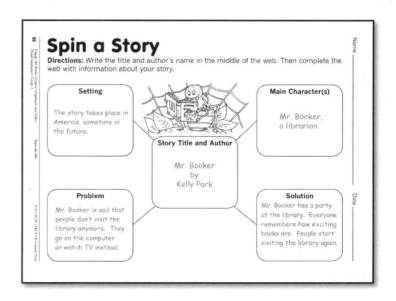

In the Spotlight: Venn Diagram

Materials

In the Spotlight reproducible

Stuart Little by E. B. White

Skills Objectives

Recognize character traits.

Distinguish between similarities and differences.

A **Venn Diagram** is a helpful tool for organizing and comparing two sets of data. It clearly divides traits into two categories—traits that are shared and traits that are not. This distinction allows comparisons to be made quickly and easily. In this activity, students use a Venn diagram to compare and contrast two story characters. Present the lesson after the class has read a book together. The activity is based on *Stuart Little*, but any familiar book will do.

1. Show the book *Stuart Little* to the class. Review with students who Stuart is and what the book is about. (Stuart is the main character. He is born into a human family, but he looks like a mouse. The book is about Stuart's many adventures.)

2. Remind students about Stuart's brother, George. Ask if the two brothers were alike or different. Allow students to share their ideas.

3. Draw two large, overlapping circles on the board to make a Venn diagram. Write *Stuart Little* over one circle and *George Little* over the other. Tell students they can use the Venn diagram to organize their comparison of the two characters.

4. Ask students to state one way that the characters are different and write the traits on the outer parts of the circles. For example, you might write *mouse* for Stuart and *human* for George.

5. Ask students to state one way that the characters are alike. Write that trait in the overlapping section of the diagram. For example, you might write *son of Mr. and Mrs. Little*.

6. Give students a copy of the **In the Spotlight reproducible (page 70)**. Tell them to complete their own Venn diagrams for Stuart and George. They can use the diagram on the board to get started. Remind students that when making comparisons, they should consider personality traits (e.g., clever, careless) and circumstances (e.g., lives in a house, lives in an apartment), as well as physical characteristics (e.g., tall, short).

7. Check students' ideas as they work on their diagrams. If students have difficulty thinking of words or phrases, ask guiding questions such as: *Would you like to have either George or Stuart as your brother? Why or why not? If George and Stuart were in your class, what kind of students would they be? Do you think they would be hard working and studious? Would they be fun to do things with?*

8. When students have completed their diagrams, compile their responses on the Venn diagram you began at the beginning of the lesson. Review all the details that make each character unique and alike.

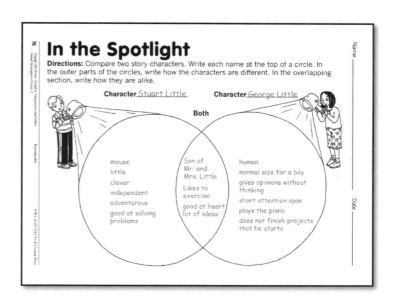

Name _____ Date _____

In the Spotlight

Directions: Compare two story characters. Write each name at the top of a circle. In the outer parts of the circles, write how the characters are different. In the overlapping section, write how they are alike.

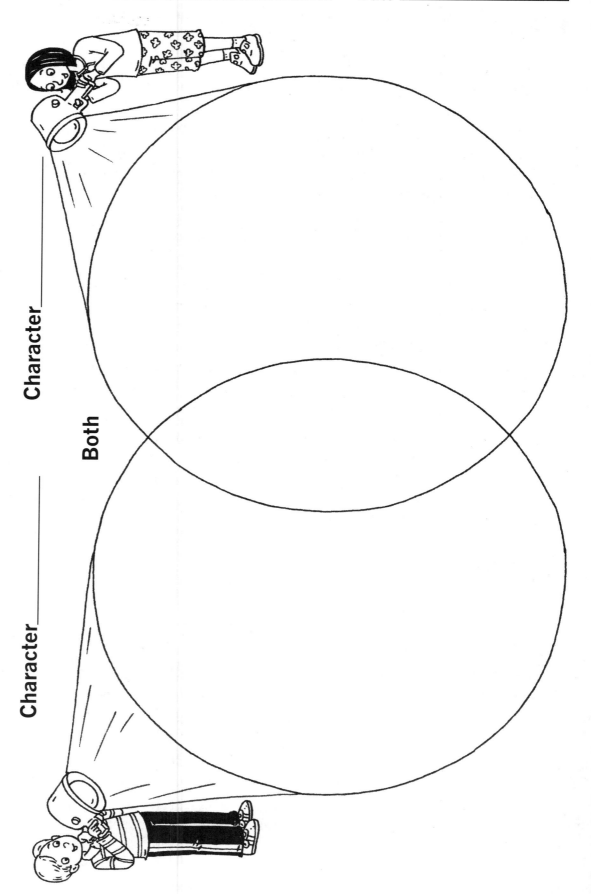

Character _____

Both

Character _____

Follow the Steps: Chain of Events Chart

Skills Objectives

Identify main events of a story.

Put events in sequential order.

Understand that a series of events leads to a final outcome.

Materials

Follow the Steps reproducible

Freckle Juice by Judy Blume

10 paper clips

A **Chain of Events Chart** displays information in sequential steps. In a literature lesson, it illustrates how a story moves from one event to the next. This activity helps students identify main events and explore plot development. The activity is based on Judy Blume's *Freckle Juice*, but any familiar book may be used.

1. Stand at the front of the classroom and start linking paper clips together. Discuss how the chain is made up of individual links. Each link is connected to the next. Explain that a story is made up of "links," too. These links are the events in the story. The events lead from one to the next until the final outcome is reached.

2. Show *Freckle Juice* to the class, and review what the book is about (a boy wants freckles). Then brainstorm several events from the story, and write students' responses on the board (e.g., *Andrew looks at Nicky's freckles. Andrew asks Nicky how he got freckles. Sharon sells Andrew a recipe for freckles.*) Make sure students include several events from the beginning, middle, and end of the story.

3. Tell students they will describe what happens in the story *Freckle Juice*; however, they can use only six main events. Have them look at the events they brainstormed and choose the one that sets the story in motion.

4. If they are not sure which sentence to pick, guide them. For example, if they are trying to decide between *Andrew looks at Nicky's freckles* and *Andrew asks Nicky about getting freckles*, help them see that the second sentence is the better choice. (This event allows Sharon to overhear the conversation and plan to trick Andrew.) Circle the appropriate sentence.

5. Give students a copy of the **Follow the Steps reproducible (page 73)**, and point out the "chain" of footprints. Point out how one footprint leads to the next. Have students copy the circled sentence onto the first footprint.

6. Let students work in pairs to fill in the remaining five sentences for the page. Remind them to choose sentences that describe main events—events that are necessary for the story's plot to move forward.

7. When they have completed their pages, invite students to share their responses with the class. As they call out sentences, circle them on the board. If students have different opinions, ask them to explain their choices.

Extended Learning

- Select one of the circled sentences on the board. Ask the class how the story would have been different if that event didn't occur. For example, if you circled the sentence *Andrew asks Nicky how he got freckles,* ask how the story would have changed if the conversation never took place.

- Discuss how a story's main events form a *summary*. Have students use their graphic organizers to write a paragraph summarizing *Freckle Juice*.

- Let students choose their own book to summarize on the Follow the Steps reproducible. Remind them that each event they choose should be important to story development.

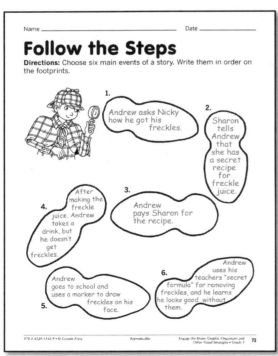

Name _____ Date _____

Follow the Steps

Directions: Choose six main events of a story. Write them in order on the footprints.

1. Andrew asks Nicky how he got his freckles.

2. Sharon tells Andrew that she has a secret recipe for freckle juice.

3. Andrew pays Sharon for the recipe.

4. After making the freckle juice, Andrew takes a drink, but he doesn't get freckles.

5. Andrew goes to school and uses a marker to draw freckles on his face.

6. Andrew uses his teachers "secret formula" for removing freckles, and he learns he looks good without them.

978-1-4129-5342-9 • © Corwin Press   Reproducible   Engage the Brain: Graphic Organizers and Other Visual Strategies • Grade 3   73

Name _____   Date _____

Follow the Steps

Directions: Choose six main events of a story. Write them in order on the footprints.

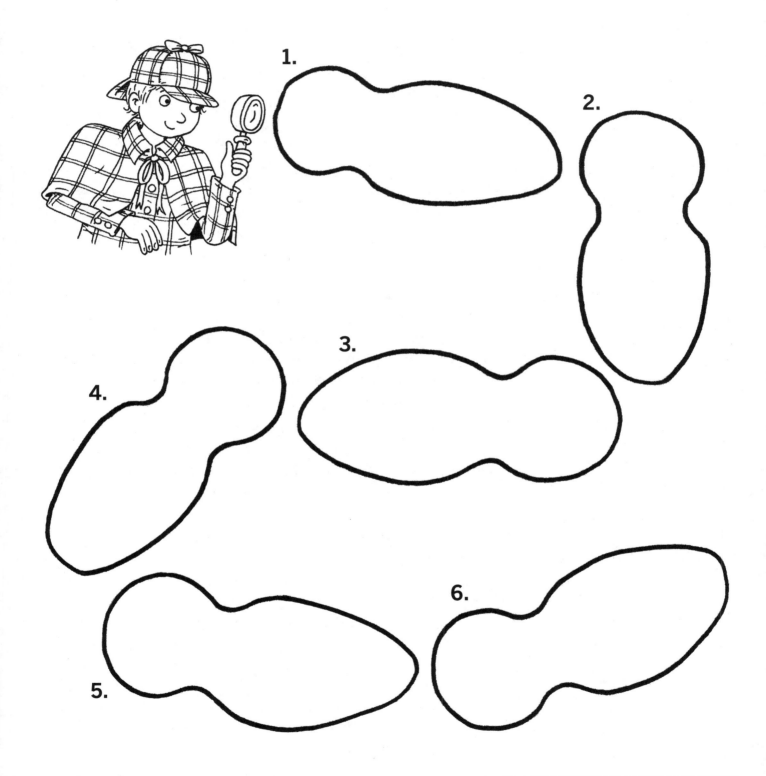

1.

2.

3.

4.

5.

6.

Fairy Tale Castle: Story Map

Materials

Fairy Tale Castle reproducible

fairy tale books

Skills Objectives

Read and analyze fairy tales.

Recognize the main characteristics of a fairy tale.

The **Story Map** used in the following activity helps students examine how fairy tales are constructed. Like fables and myths, fairy tales have distinct characteristics that set them apart from other literary genres.

1. Present a variety of fairy tales for students to read.

2. Once students are familiar with several fairy tales, talk about general characteristics they observed in the stories. Write their ideas on the board.

3. Give students a copy of the **Fairy Tale Castle reproducible (page 75)**. Compare the features on the page to students' ideas. Explain that all fairy tales share similarities, such as a hero or heroine who must overcome a problem. Explain that one or more characters often have magical powers and that fairy tales generally have a happy ending.

4. Divide the class into small groups and assign each group one of the fairy tales the class read. Instruct students to complete sections of the castle with words, phrases, or sentences. They can add pictures, too. Walk around the room as students work so you can check their progress and answer any questions.

5. Afterward, let groups share their graphic organizers with the class.

Extended Learning

Have students use the Fairy Tale Castle reproducible to plan original fairy tales. Instruct them to fill in the sections to make a story outline. Then have students write their fairy tale, using their outline as a guide.

Fairy Tale Castle

Directions: Choose a fairy tale. Fill in the castle with elements from the story.

Title of Fairy Tale — Rumpelstiltskin

Use of Magic — A stranger helps a miller's daughter spin straw into gold.

Good Characters — Miller's daughter servant

Bad Characters — Rumpelstiltskin

Happy Ending — The queen keeps her baby, and she never hears from Rumpelstiltskin again.

Problem — The miller's daughter must spin straw into gold. She gets help from a stranger, but she must give up her first child if she can't guess his name.

Solution — A servant tells the miller's daughter who is now queen that the stranger is Rumpelstiltskin. Rumpelstiltskin gets angry and goes away.

Name

Date

Name ______________________ Date ______________

Fairy Tale Castle

Directions: Choose a fairy tale. Fill in the castle with elements from the story.

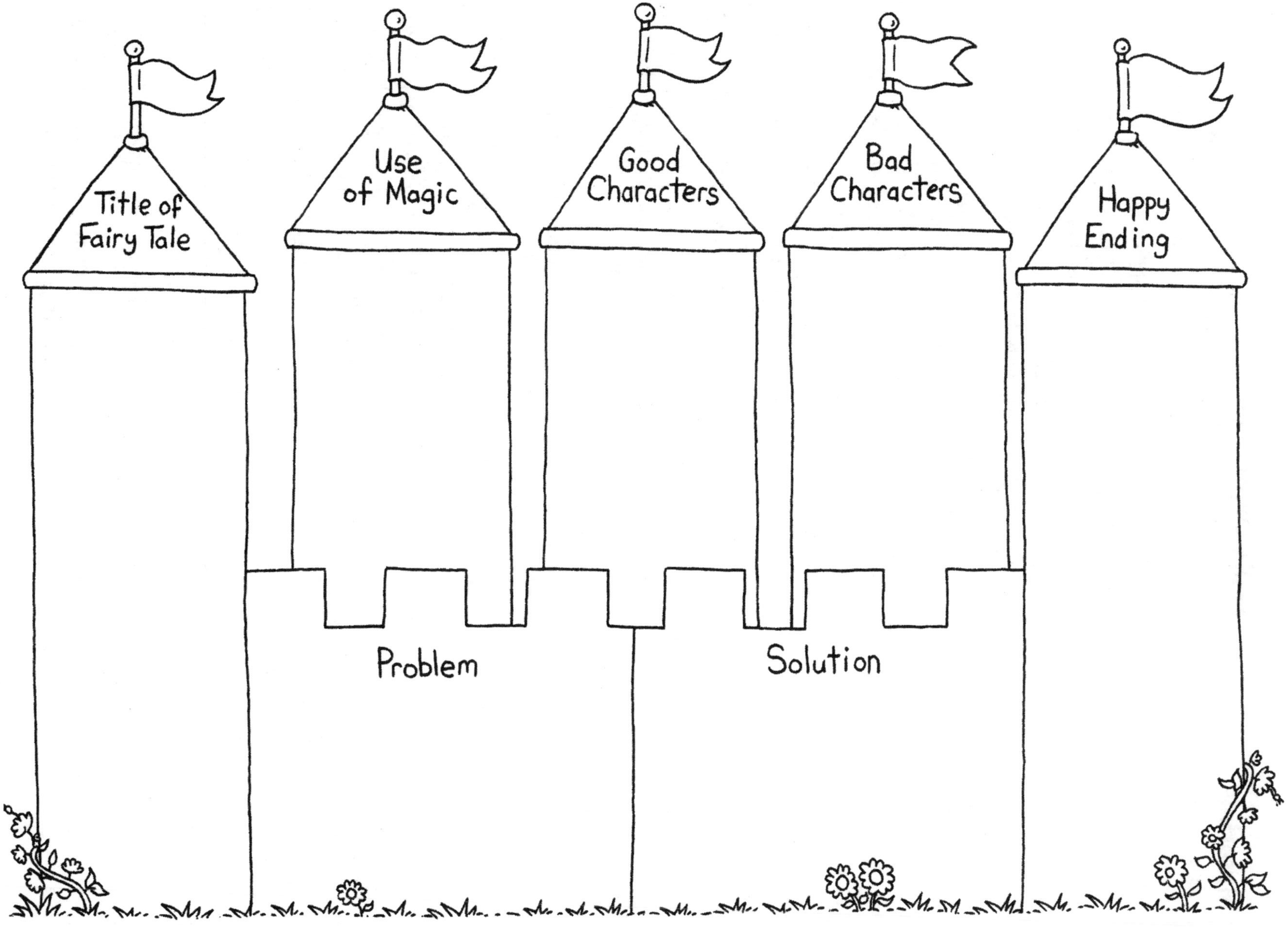

Title of Fairy Tale
Use of Magic
Good Characters
Bad Characters
Happy Ending
Problem
Solution

What a Blast! E-Chart

Materials
chart paper

Skills Objectives

Identify the main idea and supporting details in a passage.

Write a paragraph that has a clear main idea and supporting details.

An **E-Chart** is a graphic organizer that resembles a capital *E*, with the middle horizontal stem of the E extended to the left. An E-chart is an effective prewriting tool. Students write a topic or theme on the extended stem and list supporting details on the three short stems. This information allows students to write concise, cohesive paragraphs.

1. Before the lesson, copy this passage on a sheet of chart paper: *Teeth are important in many ways. You use them every day to bite or chew food. Without teeth, you couldn't munch on nuts or enjoy a fresh, juicy apple. Teeth also help you speak. Close your eyes and say the words "think," "sad," and "zoo." Did you feel your teeth work with your mouth and tongue to produce the "th," "s," and "z" sounds? You wouldn't be able to make these sounds if you didn't have teeth. Finally, teeth support the muscles around your mouth and keep your face from sagging. Healthy teeth also give you a beautiful smile and help you look terrific!*

2. Read the passage with the class. Ask students to state the main idea (teeth are important), and call on a volunteer to underline the corresponding phrase on the chart. Draw a large E on the board, and extend the middle stem out to the left to create an E-chart. On the extended stem, write the main idea: *Teeth are important.*

3. Have students read the passage again. Ask them to find details that support the idea that teeth are important and underline the appropriate phrases on the board. (*bite or chew food, help you speak, help you look terrific*) Write these supporting details on the three short horizontal stems.

	They help you bite and chew food
Teeth are important	They help you speak
	They help you look terrific

4. Explain that an E-chart can help students plan their writing. Then work with the class to write a paragraph using the E-chart to

outline the main idea and details. Begin by drawing an E-chart on the board. Have students do the same on a sheet of paper. Then write this main idea on the long horizontal stem: *A computer is a great learning tool.* Have students follow along on their papers.

5. Ask students to suggest three supporting details, and write them on the short stems. For example, students might suggest the following:
    - A computer lets you look up information quickly from many different sources.
    - A computer helps you get up-to-date information.
    - A computer can show you information in a colorful, interesting way.

6. Next, guide students to combine the main idea and details to write a cohesive paragraph. Write the paragraph on the board. For example:

    A computer is a great learning tool. For example, you can look up information quickly from many different sources. You can find information from hundreds of Web sites. A computer also helps you get up-to-date information. Library books may contain outdated information that is not longer true or helpful. A computer makes learning fun, too. You can find Web sites that show information in a colorful, interesting way. In fact, learning with a computer can seem like playing a game!

7. Have students use an E-chart to plan their own paragraphs. Begin by having them pick one of the following topics:
    - Exercise can be fun.
    - Teachers and students can learn from each other.
    - _____ is the best time of the year.
    (Fill in the blank with the name of a holiday or season.)

8. Give students a copy of the **What a Blast! reproducible (page 78)**, on which they will write the main idea and three supporting details. Instruct students to use their planning chart to write the final paragraph. As the class writes, circulate among students to make sure they stay focused on their main ideas.

9. When they're done, invite students to share their writing in small groups.

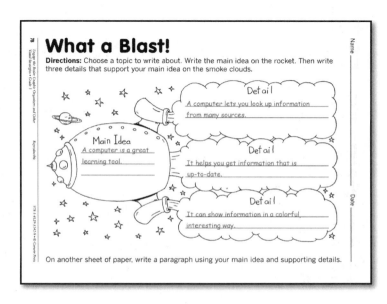

Name _____ Date _____

What a Blast!

Directions: Choose a topic to write about. Write the main idea on the rocket. Then write three details that support your main idea on the smoke clouds.

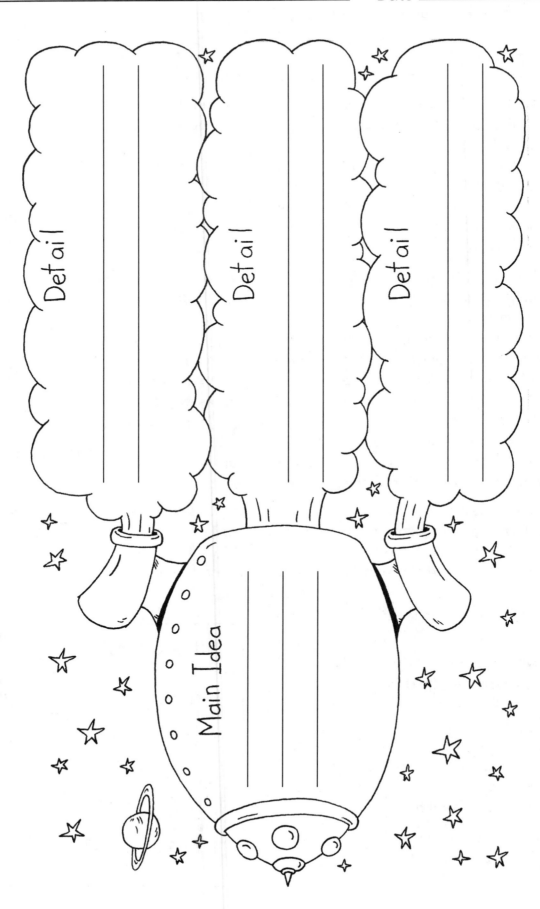

Detail

Detail

Detail

Main Idea

On another sheet of paper, write a paragraph using your main idea and supporting details.

"Paint" with Words: Word Wheel

Skills Objectives

Generate descriptive words.

Expand vocabulary.

Write effective descriptions.

Materials

Word Wheel reproducible

apples

Descriptive writing can be a difficult skill to master. First, the writer needs to choose words carefully to convey an accurate image of the subject. Second, the writer needs to provide enough detail to present a complete picture of the subject. Students often have problems with both requirements. You can help by giving them opportunities to examine a subject up close before writing about it. You can also provide a graphic organizer, such as a **Word Wheel**, that allows students to collect descriptive words as a prewriting activity.

1. Hold up an apple, and ask the class to describe it. Students may suggest words such as *round* and *red*. Tell them to use more than just their sense of sight. Then divide the class into small groups, and give an apple to each group.

2. Give students a copy of the **Word Wheel reproducible (page 81)**. Tell them to draw their apple in the middle of the wheel.

3. Instruct students to examine their apple and think about how it looks, feels, and smells. Tell them to imagine biting into the apple and think about how it might taste or sound.

4. Invite group members to work together to fill in each section of the wheel. Remind them to write words and phrases that relate to as many senses as they can. For example, *red* refers to sight, while *crunchy* refers to sound.

5. Later, ask students to share their ideas, while you list them on the board. Then have them close their eyes as you read aloud from the list. As you read, invite students to visualize the apple in their minds.

6. Have students open their eyes. Discuss the different senses to which the words and phrases you read appealed. Explain that in order to write a good description, students must use specific words that help paint pictures in the minds of the reader or listener.

Extended Learning

- Have students use the words they generated to create a descriptive poem about an apple. The poems may or may not rhyme. Following are two examples:

  Crisp and crunchy,
  Red and sweet,
  A smooth, shiny apple
  Is delicious to eat.

  Round and crimson,
  Cool in my hands,
  Pleasant to hold,
  Juicy, sweet, delicious.

- Let students choose their own small objects to study, such as another fruit, a leaf, or a toy. Then give them a copy of the Word Wheel reproducible. They can fill in the wheel with colorful, interesting words. Then invite students to read their words in small groups. As they read, instruct other group members to close their eyes and visualize the object being described.

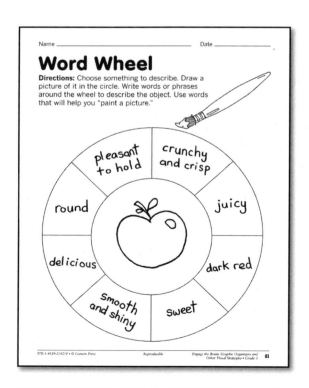

Word Wheel

Directions: Choose something to describe. Draw a picture of it in the circle. Write words or phrases around the wheel to describe the object. Use words that will help you "paint a picture."

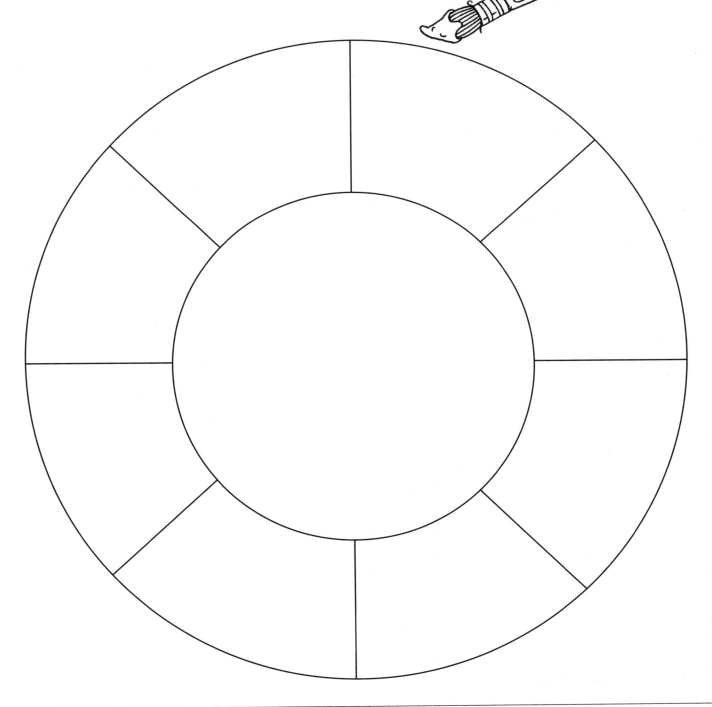

Spell It! Sorting Trays Organizer

Materials
Spell It! Sorting Trays reproducible

Skills Objectives
Plan a strategy for learning spelling words.
Use spelling words in context.

Part of a student's learning process is mastering new material. In this activity, **Sorting Trays** provide a concrete, visual way for students to categorize *sorting trays* into two groups—words they can spell easily and those they cannot. Once difficult words have been identified, students can spend time mastering them.

1. Each Monday, give a pretest of the spelling words for the week. Explain to students that the pretest will help them separate the words they already know how to spell from those they need to practice.

2. Immediately after the pretest, review the answers with students. Write the words on the board as students check their work.

3. Give students a copy of the **Spell It! Sorting Trays reproducible (page 83)**. On the top tray, have them list words they spelled correctly. On the bottom tray, have them list misspelled words. Students can keep the sheet for reference during spelling activities. (See Step 4.)

4. Add the following activities to your week's regular spelling assignments:
   - Have students make flashcards of words they spelled incorrectly. Pair up students and have partners test each other.
   - Ask students to write sentences using words they spelled incorrectly, and highlight the words so they stand out. Discuss any outstanding features that might help students remember the correct spelling.

5. At the end of the week, give your usual spelling test. Pass back the graded tests and have students compare their results with the pretest. If students still have problems, invite them to review words with you.

Spell It! Sorting Trays

Directions: On the top tray, write the words you know how to spell. On the bottom tray, write the words you need to practice.

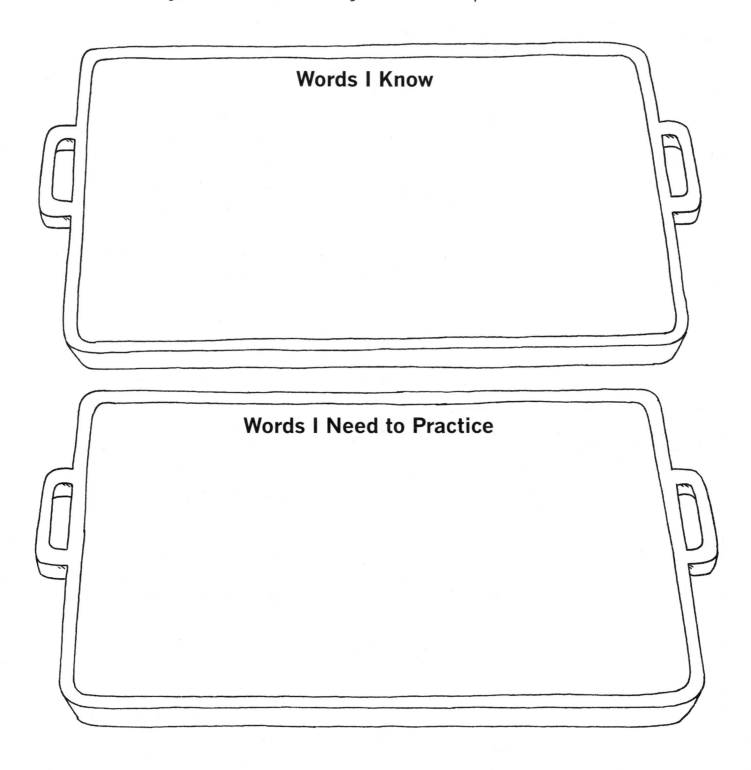

Words I Know

Words I Need to Practice

CHAPTER 5

Physical Education, Art, and Music

Invent a New Game: Outline Chart

Skills Objectives

Create an original game.

Recognize the components that make a good game.

Take time in your P.E. classes to foster creativity as well as physical activity. In this activity, students work together to invent original games or modify existing ones. They use an **Outline Chart** to list the main components of their game so they can test and refine the game.

1. Show the class a basketball, and ask students what sport it represents. Explain that basketball was invented in 1891 by James Naismith, a Massachusetts college P.E. instructor. Winters get very cold in Massachusetts, so the P.E. department head asked Naismith to create a team sport that could be played indoors. Naismith used a soccer ball and two peach baskets, which were attached to a balcony railing ten feet above the floor. Basketball quickly became popular. Eventually, metal hoops replaced the baskets and basketballs replaced the soccer balls.

2. Challenge students to invent a new P.E. game for elementary school students. Brainstorm a list of characteristics they would like their game to have (e.g., *has to be fun, easy to play, played in teams, involves a lot of running*).

3. Divide the class into groups of three or four. Then take students to an open area and display a variety of sports equipment. Inform groups that they may use one or more pieces of equipment, or they may invent a game, like tag, that uses none. They also may modify an existing game, like soccer or shadow tag. Give groups time to devise the format and rules. Assist groups as needed.

4. Then let students test their games. Give them a copy of the **A New Game reproducible (page 85)**. Have groups fill in the charts and play their game several times to check that they provided adequate directions.

5. During the next several P.E. periods, invite groups to teach their games to the class. Have students refer to their charts as they describe the games.

Name _____   Date _____

A New Game

Directions: Invent a game for your class. Write about it on the chart.

Name of Game	Number of Players
Equipment Needed	
How to Play	
Rules to Remember	

Jog and Walk: Record Chart

Materials

Jog and Walk Record reproducible

Skills Objectives

Set a goal for jogging and walking.
Keep a record of laps completed each week.

Encourage students to keep physically active by working toward a goal as a class. Jogging and walking are two activities students can do on a regular basis at school. Keeping a **Record Chart** to track their progress motivates students to stay on task.

1. At the beginning of a P.E. period, discuss the importance of keeping active. Brainstorm ways that physical activity helps us stay healthy.

2. Tell students that jogging and walking are two activities they can do at school to strengthen their hearts and lungs. They will make jogging or walking part of their school routine.

3. Take students outdoors where they can jog or walk. Choose a place, such as the perimeter of a playground or field, where you can count laps. Then briskly walk around the area. Tell students to keep track of the number of laps they complete.

4. Back in the classroom, give students a copy of the **Jog and Walk Record reproducible (page 87)**. Tell students to fill in the information at the top of the chart, including what the square represents (one lap around the area) and the dates. Have students color one square for each lap completed.

5. Place the charts in a file folder. During the week, take students out to jog or walk as often as possible. Have them record how many laps they complete. Each Friday, total the number of laps.

6. Every week, pass out new copies of the Jog and Walk Record, and challenge students to increase the number of laps. To make the exercise more fun, calculate the distance of each lap, and then figure out the total distance students cover in a week and a month.

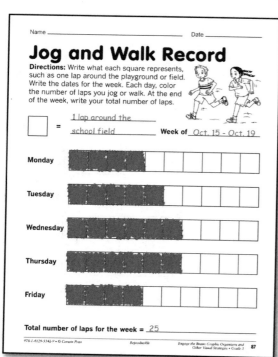

Jog and Walk Record

Directions: Write what each square represents, such as one lap around the playground or field. Write the dates for the week. Each day, color the number of laps you jog or walk. At the end of the week, write your total number of laps.

☐ = _____

_____ **Week of** _____

Monday

Tuesday

Wednesday

Thursday

Friday

Total number of laps for the week = _____

Larger-Than-Life Flowers: Models

Materials

photos of Georgia O'Keeffe's flower paintings (available in library books, postcards, and calendars)

artificial or real flowers

magnifying glasses

tempera paint

paintbrushes

large painting paper

newspaper

Skills Objectives

Make observations.

Create a painting based on close-up observations.

Georgia O'Keeffe was known for her vibrant paintings of flowers. She wanted people to notice a flower's beauty by painting huge, close-up views, filling the entire canvas. Using O'Keeffe's work as a **Model**, invite students to examine flowers and paint them larger than life. As students study the fine details of each flower, they will discover natural beauty as O'Keeffe did.

1. Show students some of Georgia O'Keeffe's flower paintings. Ask them to describe her work. For example: *The colors are bright. The flowers are very large. It feels as if you are looking deep inside each flower.*

2. Ask guiding questions to help students think about the effect of O'Keeffe's flower paintings on the observer: *Do the paintings make flowers look attractive or ugly? How do you think O'Keeffe felt about flowers? Do you think the artist wants other people to notice flowers?*

3. Discuss how the flowers cover the entire canvas. Ask why the artist may have done this. (She wanted people to notice the beauty and wonder of flowers and be as impressed with nature as she was.)

4. Tell students they will be painting larger-than-life flowers in the style of O'Keeffe. Then divide the class into small groups and provide each group with magnifying glasses and a variety of artificial or real flowers. As students examine the flowers, have them look for things they may not have noticed before, such as a flower's delicate inner structures or its varying shades of colors.

5. Have each student choose a flower to paint. Then distribute painting materials and cover the work area with newspaper. Have students paint their flowers so they fill the whole paper. Place O'Keeffe's work around the room for inspiration.

6. When the paintings have dried, hang them around the room for a brilliant display! Invite students to guess which kinds of flowers appear in the paintings.

Life of an Artist: Timeline

Skills Objectives
Research an artist.
Identify main events in the artist's life.
Write events in sequential order.

A **Timeline** presents events in chronological order. In this activity, students research famous artists and learn about their contributions. They present the main events of each artist's life on a timeline, and then use the timeline as a reference for writing a final report.

1. Display works of famous artists. Include different art forms, such as paintings, ceramics, sculptures, and collages. Discuss how art enriches people's lives.

2. Tell students that the artists we all know of were not always famous. Though some were successful in their lifetimes, many were mocked because their art did not reflect contemporary views.

3. Tell students they will be researching the lives of famous artists. Provide children's books, encyclopedias, and other reference materials. Have students look through the materials and choose an artist to research. Provide ample time (up to a week) for students to read the materials and take notes.

4. After students complete their research, distribute the **Life of an Artist reproducible (page 90)**. Have them write the name of their chosen artist at the top of the page. Point out that the paint palettes form a timeline to help them organize information in chronological order.

5. Direct students to look at their notes and circle the six most important dates and events to put on the timeline. Remind them to choose events that provide a good understanding of who the artist was and how he or she came to acquire a distinctive style. As students work on their timelines, check that they are selecting appropriate events.

6. Have students use their timelines to write reports about their artists. Distribute copies of the **Famous Artist Report reproducible (page 91)**, and have students elaborate on the events from their timelines.

7. When reports are completed, invite students to present them to the class.

Materials
Life of an Artist reproducible

Famous Artist Report reproducible

pictures of artists' works (from library books, posters, and calendars)

reference materials for researching artists' lives, such as Mike Venezia's *Getting to Know the World's Greatest Artists* series (Children's Press)

Name ______________________________ Date ______________

Life of an Artist

Directions: Write the name of an artist on the top line. Then choose six events from the artist's life. Write the year each event occurred, and then describe the event.

Life of: ____

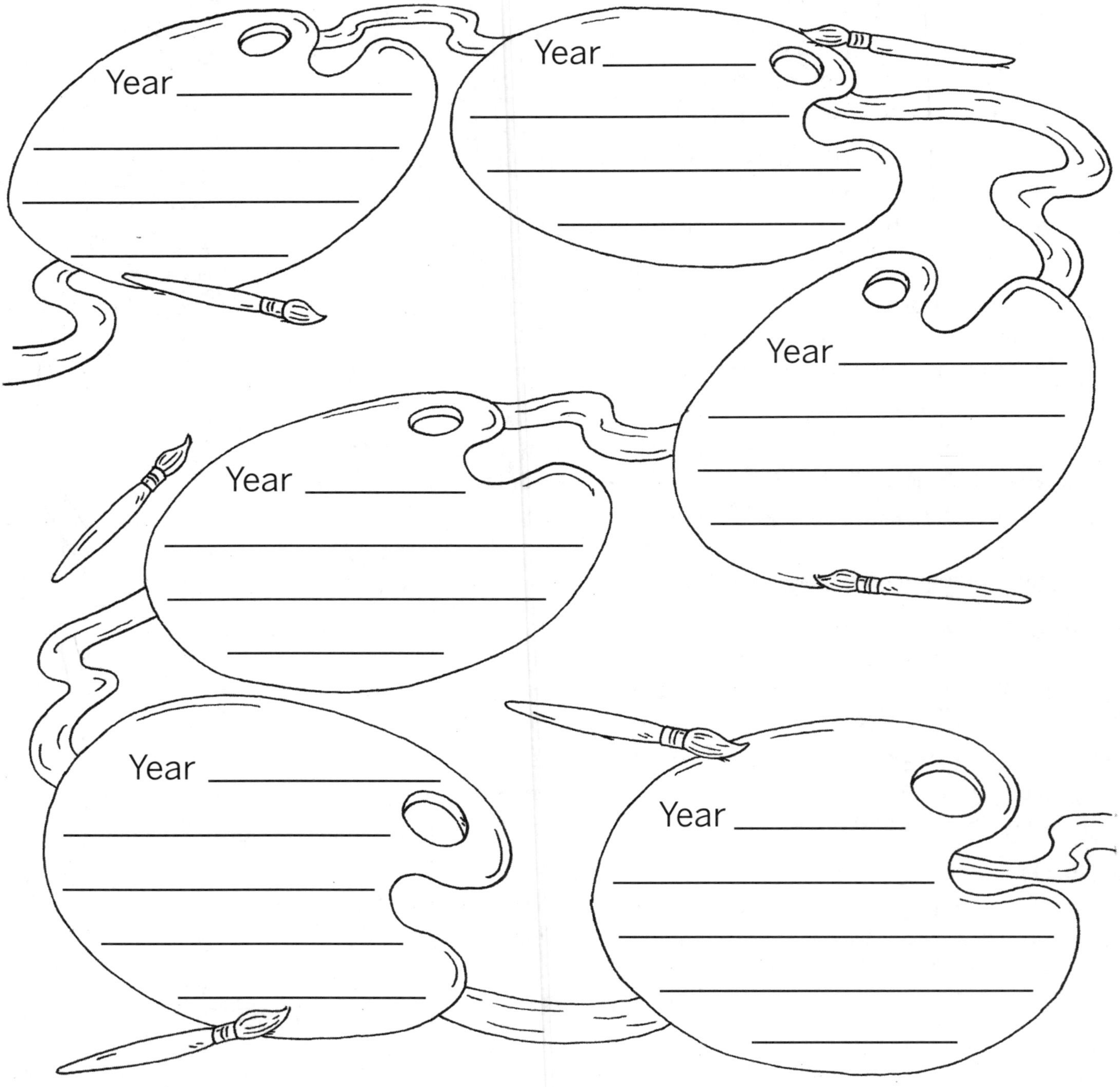

Year
Year
Year
Year
Year
Year

Name _____ Date _____

Famous Artist Report

Directions: Write the name of the artist at the top of the paint palette. Then write your report below.

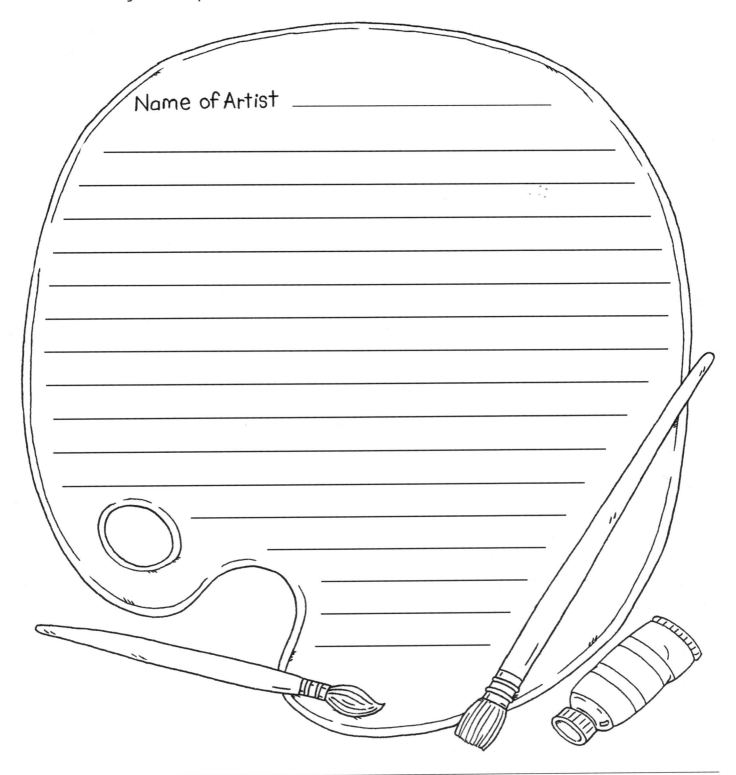

Name of Artist _____

Music in My World: Four-Column Chart

Materials

Music in My World reproducible

radio

chart paper

Skills Objectives

Recognize that music has many purposes.
Keep track of when and where music is played.

Music is an important part of our everyday lives. It is all around us, on television, radios, and CDs, and is featured in all kinds of celebrations. In this activity, students use a **Four-Column Chart** to keep track of when and where they hear music in a single day. They will discover the many different situations and reasons for which music is played.

1. Turn on the radio, and ask students to identify the music playing. Invite them to share other times they hear music (e.g., *on a CD; on television; at a birthday party, wedding, or restaurant*). Ask why the music was played (e.g., *to celebrate a special time, to relax people*). Help students see that music is played in many situations for many purposes.

2. Tell students to be on the "lookout" for music the rest of the day. Give them a copy of the **Music in My World reproducible (page 93)**. Point out the columns on the chart where they will write the time they hear music, where they are when they hear the music, where the music is coming from (e.g., TV, CD, live performance), and the purpose of the music (e.g., relaxation, entertainment). Have them begin at school and complete their charts at home.

3. When students bring their charts back to school, compile their responses on a sheet of chart paper. Discuss the many everyday situations in which music is played. Invite students to share how different music makes them feel.

Music in My World

Directions: Keep track of when and where you hear music all day. Write the information in the chart.

Date: March 18

Time	Where were you?	Where was the music coming from?	What was the purpose of the music? (Examples: relaxation, entertainment)
11:00 am	at school	music class	learn new songs for a concert
3:45 pm	in the car	the radio	make the ride home more interesting
4:30 pm	in the dentist's office	a CD	make people more relaxed
7:00 pm	watching TV	the TV show	theme song helps people recognize the show
7:15 pm	watching TV	TV commercial	get people's attention an help people remember
8:30 pm	at home	a CD	relax before going to sleep

Music in My World

Directions: Keep track of when and where you hear music all day. Write the information in the chart.

Date: _____

Time	Where were you?	Where was the music coming from?	What was the purpose of the music? (Examples: relaxation, entertainment)

A Medley of Musical Words: Graphic Chart

Materials

Musical Words reproducible

CD or audiocassette of familiar music

CD or tape player

Skills Objectives

Expand vocabulary.
Understand musical terms.

Learning musical terms will help students better understand and appreciate the nature of music. In this activity, they record musical vocabulary on a **Graphic Chart**.

1. Play a familiar song for students. Then ask them to hum the tune. Explain that the tune of a piece of music is called a *melody*. Write the word on the board, along with its definition.

2. Have students quickly sing the first verse of the song together. Then have them sing the verse more slowly. Ask how the two verses differed. Explain that the speed of a piece of music is called *tempo*. Add the word and definition to the board.

3. Next, tell students to imagine that one singer performed the song. Explain that a *solo* is a performance by one person. Write the word and its definition on the board.

4. Tell students that a performance by two musicians is called a *duet*, and write the word and its definition on the board. Continue to introduce and discuss the terms *trio* and *harmony*.

5. Give students a copy of the **Musical Words reproducible (page 95)**. Tell them to write the terms they've learned on the musical notes and the definitions on the corresponding lines.

6. As students' knowledge of music grows, let students write new terms on additional copies of the Musical Words reproducible. Review the words by incorporating them into future lessons. Create opportunities for students to use the terms when describing a musical piece or discussing a performance.

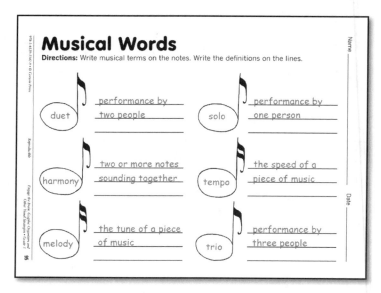

Name _____ Date _____

Musical Words

Directions: Write musical terms on the notes. Write the definitions on the lines.

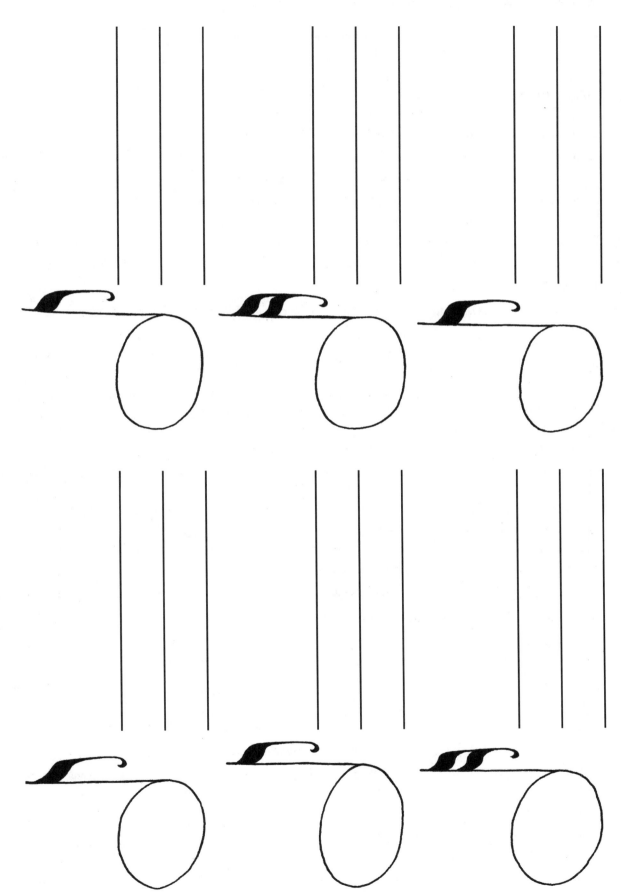

References

Byrne, J. M. (2002). Seed. In *World book encyclopedia* (Vol. 17, pp. 281–284). Chicago, IL: World Book.

Chronology of the life of Mary Cassatt. Retrieved December 9, 2006, from http://www.nga.gov/collection/cassattchron.shtm.

Col, Ja. (n.d.). *Graphic organizers.* Retrieved September 18, 2006, from the Enchanted Learning Web site:http://www.enchantedlearning.com/graphicorganizers/.

Cooney, B. (1982). *Miss Rumphius.* New York, NY: Puffin Books.

Farndon, J. (1992). *How the earth works.* London, England: Dorling Kindersley.

Fixico, D. L. (2002). Indian, American. In *World book encyclopedia* (Vol. 10, pp. 158–160). Chicago, IL: World Book.

Gallery, D., & Gallery, M. (n.d.). *Graphic organizers.* Retrieved September 18, 2006, from the Enchanted Learning Web site: http://www.enchantedlerning.com/graphicorganizers/.

Gardner, H. (1983). Frames of mind: *The theory of multiple intelligences.* New York, NY: Basic Books.

Head, J. W. (2002). Venus. In *World book encyclopedia* (Vol. 20, pp. 310–314). Chicago, IL: World Book.

Jensen, E., & Johnson, G. (1994). *The learning brain.* San Diego, CA: Turning Point for Teachers.

Longyear, R. M. (2002). Music. In *World book encyclopedia* (Vol. 13, pp. 946–954). Chicago, IL: World Book.

MacDonald, F. (1992). *Plains Indians.* New York, NY: Barron's.

McCarthy, B. (1990). Using the 4MAT system to bring learning styles to schools. *Educational Leadership, 48* (2), 31–37.

National Council for the Social Studies. (2002). *Expectations of excellence: Curriculum standards for social studies.* Silver Spring, MD: National Council for the Social Studies (NCSS).

National Council of Teachers of English and International Reading Association. (1996). *Standards for the English language arts.* Urbana, IL: National Council of Teachers of English (NCTE).

National Council of Teachers of Mathematics. (2005). *Principles and standards for school mathematics.* Reston, VA: National Council of Teachers of Mathematics (NCTM).

National Research Council. (2005). *National science education standards.* Washington, DC: National Academy Press.

Ogle, D. M. (2000). Make it visual: A picture is worth a thousand words. In M. McLaughlin & M. Vogt (Eds.), *Creativity and innovation in content area teaching.* Norwood, MA: Christopher-Gordon.

Oxlade, C. (1994). *Inventions.* New York, NY: Zigzag Publishing.

Pasachoff, J. M. (2002). Planet. In *World book encyclopedia* (Vol. 15, pp. 507–514). Chicago, IL: World Book.

Reynolds, J. S. (2002). Invention. In *World book encyclopedia* (Vol. 10, pp. 354–364). Chicago, IL: World Book.

Sewall, M. (1986). *The Pilgrims of Plimoth.* New York, NY: Aladdin Paperbacks.

Smith, W. (2002). Flag. In *World book encyclopedia* (Vol. 7, pp. 192–214). Chicago, IL: World Book.

Spinrad, H. (2002). Mercury. In *World book encyclopedia* (Vol. 13, pp. 414–416). Chicago, IL: World Book.

Tate, M. L. (2003). *Worksheets don't grow dendrites: 20 instructional strategies that engage the brain.* Thousand Oaks, CA: Corwin Press.

Thompson, J. R. (2002). Basketball. In *World book encyclopedia* (Vol. 2, pp. 151–152). Chicago, IL: World Book.

Van de Walle, J. A. (2004). Helping children master the basic facts. *Elementary and middle school mathematics: Teaching developmentally* (pp. 156–177). Boston, MA: Pearson Education.

VanCleave, J. (1990). *Biology for every kid.* New York, NY: John Wiley & Sons.

Venezia, M. (1993). *Georgia O'Keeffe.* Chicago, IL: Childrens Press.

Venezia, M. (1993). *Mary Cassatt.* Danbury, Chicago, IL: Childrens Press.

Wortel, J. P. (2002). Teeth. In *World book encyclopedia* (Vol. 19, pp. 433–435). Chicago, IL: World Book.